MW01490588

1

Contents

JAPAN
WHAT TO SEE

Mount Fuji
Visit the active volcano and highest mountain in Japan.

Honshu Island

Okinawa Churaumi Aquarium
Play with dolphins at this huge, family-friendly aquarium.

Motobu

Jigokudani Monkey Park
Witness the snow monkeys descend from the steep cliffs and sit in the hot springs.

Yamanouchi

Kinkakuji
Visit the garden complex of the Zen Buddhist Temple of the Golden Pavilion.

Kyoto

Niseko
Take in the mountain ranges and ski the powder at one of Japan's best resorts.

Niseko

Himeji Castle
One of Japan's best-preserved samurai castles.

Hyogo Prefecture

Phoenix Hall at Byodo-in Temple
Regarded as Japan's most beautiful and elegant building.

Uji City

Dogo Onsen
One of the oldest onsen hot springs in Japan.

Matsuyama

JAPAN
SHOPPING

Candy
At the forefront of Japanese style, this store houses both new and used clothing.

Tokyo

Harcoza
Find an eclectic selection of accessories and enjoy the crazy interior design of this fashion store.

Tokyo

Aquvii
Offers an array of trinkets and accessories.

Tokyo

Kitakore
This mini mall is filled with designers who create one-off pieces.

Tokyo

Nan Nan Town
Visit the large-scale underground shopping facility, offering fashion and interior design pieces.

Osaka

Shinsaibashi-Suji
One of the oldest and most well-known shopping districts in the city.

Osaka

Umeda Shopping Arcade
A series of connected, underground shopping malls selling books, fashion and food.

Osaka

Crysta Nagahori
Waterfalls and glass ceilings give shoppers the feel of being above ground despite its underground reality. Conveniently linked to public transport.

Osaka

Welcome!

Japan is a treasure-trove of amazing and unique experiences. There's breathtaking landscape, awe-inspiring temples, world-famous cuisine... there's something for everyone and a new discovery every time you visit.

To get you started, here are **ten of our favourite experiences you must do in Japan** – as voted by our local insiders.

Tokyo

Kyoto

Osaka

Hiroshima

Okinawa

66 99

Breathtaking landscape, awe-inspiring temples, world-famous cuisine.

Explore the Bamboo Forest of Arashiyama

There's plenty to do around Kyoto's western suburb of **Arashiyama**, but none as famous (or as Instagram-friendly) as the **Bamboo Forest**. Stroll through its tall bamboos, visit **Nonomiya Shrine** and try to catch sight of the cheeky locals – the Macaque monkeys.

5

Stay at a traditional Ryokan

Though slightly pricier than other accommodation options, these uniquely Japanese inns offer a glimpse into Japan's rich cultural heritage. Often accompanied with *tatami* beds and a traditional Japanese breakfast, many Ryokans will also have an in-house onsen for guests. Just make sure you brush up on your onsen etiquette.

Go Scuba diving in Okinawa

Okinawa is known as Japan's Hawaii, with white sand beaches and clear blue waters teeming with life. If you're a diver, you'll be spoilt for choice here. One place on top of our dive list is **Yonagui**, an ancient underwater rock formation shrouded in mystery. Some say it's natural, truthers claim aliens. Either way, it's worth seeing for yourself.

Try Okonomiyaki fresh off the grill

Originating from Osaka, this tasty (and surprisingly filling) street food can be found nationwide. This grilled, savoury pancake, is made of a thin layer of batter mixed with shredded cabbage and

topped with your choice of ingredients. Popular toppings include green onion, pork belly or octopus (its name does literally mean "your choice grill") and it's all drizzled in a savoury-sweet sauce. *Itadakimasu!*

Visit Hiroshima Peace Park

History gets pretty real in the park's **Peace Memorial Museum**, with exhibits of burnt-out school uniforms of kids who disappeared after the attack, and photos of *hibakusha*, people who were exposed to the bomb's radiation. It's a difficult museum to see, but it carries an important message of hope for a more peaceful future.

Visit Kiyomizu-dera Temple during cherry blossom festival

Built on the site of Kyoto's **Otowa Waterfall**, the "Temple of Pure Water" is best known for its distinctive wooden

> 66 99
> **Ryokans offer a glimpse into Japan's rich cultural heritage.**

experience from a market visit through to enjoying a home-cooked meal at your host's home.

Karaoke in Tokyo
Because, well… you're in Japan. Find yourself a *nomihodai*, a Japanese all-you-can-drink bar with karaoke, and channel your inner diva.

Hike Mt Fuji
During its climbing season (early July to mid-September), this iconic, 3,776m volcano, attracts up to 10,000 people per day. The hike takes about 4-8h to reach the top and half that time to come back down. The views here are legendary for a reason. If you want to escape the busy hiking trials and just enjoy the sights of Mt. Fuji, you could also opt to hike **Mt. Ashitaka**, **Mt. Kuro** or **Mt. Ryuu-ga-take**, to experience it in all its beauty.

❝❞
You'll want to bring an extra memory card for the camera.

stage. Built in 780, it rises 13m above the hillside below and is built entirely without nails. Though its impressive architecture draws crowds all year round, we recommend going during the cherry blossom season, or late autumn, when it bursts with stunning colour. You'll want to bring an extra memory card for the camera.

Cycle around Ohara
The village of Ohara is just 20km north of Kyoto and is best explored by bicycle. It's a relatively easy route that should take around 2h, with some uphill climbs, but you'll be rewarded with picturesque rural views. Once here, explore the temple complex at **Sanzenin,** browse the quaint shops selling local crafts and don't miss the scenic **Otonoashi Waterfall**. There are also a few hot spring inns here if you want to stay the night.

Learn to make Japanese cuisine
The best way to learn to cook authentic Japanese food is to spend some time with a home cook. Sites like **Nagomi Visit** and **Traveling Spoon** can connect you with a local host and get the full

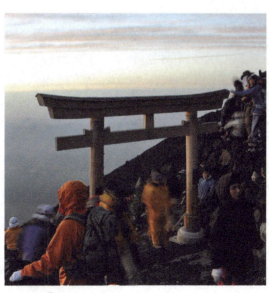

Japanese Cuisine

Japanese food is rightfully famous, and *washoku* – or Japanese cuisine – was even named a UNESCO intangible cultural heritage item in 2014. Rich in flavours and nutrients, traditional Japanese cuisine is based around super-fresh, seasonal produce.

Main dishes

Most travellers would have tried **sushi**, but, oh, that's just the beginning. If you love seafood, **sashimi** – raw, thinly sliced seafood and other meats – is a must, especially in seaside destinations like Hiroshima and Fukuoka.

If cooked and warm foods are more your thing, **ramen**, **udon**, and **soba** are the three main wheat-based noodle dishes found across Japan. All three can be served in a bowl of hot noodle soup, but soba can also be served cold. These all go great with a fresh plate of lightly-fried **Tempura**. These batter-coated seafood or fresh vegetables are served with a soy-flavoured dipping sauce, or floated in a bowl of noodles.

Speaking of warming broths, don't miss **shabu-shabu**, a decadent dish where platters of marbled meats, vegetables and noodles are cooked in a bubbling broth at the table. It's perfect for the winter months. As are **Tonkatsu**, breaded and deep-fried pork cutlets, laid over a bed of rice and can be drizzled in **Japanese curry**.

"

Most travellers would have tried sushi, but, oh, that's just the beginning.

Japanese street food

Don't even get us started with the street food. **Yakitori**, chargrilled skewers of meat, perfect with an ice-cold Asahi Beer, are served in *izakayas* and street stalls everywhere. **Okonomiyaki** and **Takoyaki** = savoury pancakes and flavoured batter balls with octopus, respectively = are also local favourites.

Desserts and sweets

Sweet treats are a big part of Japanese food culture. **Taiyaki**, a fish-shaped waffle with a variety of sweet fillings such as red beans, custard, and chocolate are a traditional favourite. It's often sold at festivals alongside **Daifuku**, a chewy rice cake filled with red bean paste. Finally, you can't miss **matcha**, or green tea, one of Japan's most famous products, which are available in a variety of sweets, snacks and confectionaries.

Cultural Highlights

With a history dating back to the 7th century BCE, Japan has a rich and multi-faceted cultural heritage. Despite the country's famous love of modernity, it has still managed to keep many of its traditions alive. Travellers can explore millennia-old shrines and temples, only a stone's throw away from the city's dizzying skyscrapers.

Shintoism and Buddhism in Japan

Though often regarded as a private, family affair, Shintoism and Buddhism teachings permeate Japanese social and cultural values. That's why you'll see Shinto shrines and Buddhist temples happily coinciding next to each other. You'll also notice its influences in architecture, art and design throughout Japan's history.

Despite its influences, religion is rarely discussed in everyday life. Most people turn to religious rituals only during key moments of celebration, such as birth, marriage, and death.

Another, more joyous celebration of religion are the many colourful *matsuri*, or festivals, that take place around the country and throughout the year.

Kabuki and Noh theatre

Originating in the 15th Century, **Kabuki theatre** is a truly avant-garde art form and one of the country's oldest forms of entertainment. Generally consisting of all male actors, Kabuki is a highly-polished performance, distinctive due to their extravagant make up, elaborate backdrops, and unique Japanese musical instruments.

Noh, on the other hand, is less radical, with less extravagant make up, scene changes, and backdrops. Due to its Shinto origins and its historic performance in shrines, it's much more serene, simplistic, and really quite a spiritual experience, centered around masks and rhythm.

Sumo match

This experience is only around during three major tournaments of the year, in January, May & September. Tokyo's **Ryogoku Kokugikan** is the major venue. Make sure you get your tickets early, though, as they sell out quick!

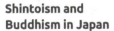

People turn to religious rituals only during key moments of celebration.

9

6699

Contrary to Hollywood belief, Geishas were never courtesans.

Onsen and hot springs

Onsen have long been used as communal bath houses, and as venues for healing and recreation. Today, the widespread availability of personal bath-tubs and showers, coupled with the hectic lifestyles of modern Japanese, have contributed to the decline of onsen as daily cleaning facilities. However, they are still famed and widely used for their healing capabilities, which vary depending on the type and composition of the onsen.

Onsens are all over Japan, but if you're looking for something a little more special, it's best to get out of the main cities. Traditional onsen locations such as **Hakone** outside Tokyo and **Beppu** in the more southerly **Oita Prefecture** are always great choices.

If your trip doesn't line up with one of these tournaments, you can always attend a morning training session instead. Just be on your best behaviour, as the requirements to watch are quite strict with audiences.

Geisha and maiko

Contrary to Hollywood belief, **Geishas** were never courtesans. Instead, working alongside the oldest profession, Geishas sought to provide entertainment through the art of conversation, charm, music, dance and poetry.

And while we're debunking myths, the popular image of an elegant figure with white make-up, red lips, elaborate hairstyles and ornate kimonos is actually more typical of a *maiko* – a trainee geisha. Fully-qualified geishas (or *geiko*) are likely more subdued, relying on their skills and charm, rather than appearance, to entertain.

If you want to catch a glimpse of these elegant creatures, you're most likely to find them in Kyoto's high-end dinners, private parties and special events to add a special touch to the proceedings.

Etiquette and Faux Pas

Respecting unwritten social rules is rooted in Japanese culture, but it can be tricky for travellers to pick up. Here are a few quick tips to help you to avoid the label of a *gaijin*, a bumbling foreigner or outsider.

Don't wear shoes indoors

This is the most common mistake. There's a reason the entrance of each house has a spot for your shoes. Some restaurants might ask you to do the same too, so make sure your socks have no holes.

Toilets are generally regarded as "unclean" areas, so many homes and even some public toilets have slippers lined up at their entrances. Just make sure you use these when you're inside the toilet area only!

Blowing your nose is... rude?

Believe it or not, sniffling is preferred over blowing your nose in public. If you *have* to blow your nose, find a private spot like the toilet. The idea of blowing your nose is repulsive to some. It goes without saying, hold onto your tissues until you find a bin.

Train etiquette

Never barge your way onto the train. Platforms have markings that show where to form orderly queues while you wait and always let others disembark before you get on.

Once you're on board, try to keep noise to a minimum. Loud behaviour is usually frowned upon because it invades others' space. Avoid talking on the phone (put it on silent mode) and send messages instead.

There are also designated seats for the elderly, injured, pregnant women, and those with young children – don't be rude and sit in them if there's someone who obviously fit one of these categories.

Behaving on the streets

You might be in a rush, but don't eat on the go. Sitting while eating shows one appreciates their food.

Smoking on the street is illegal too. Instead, head towards a clearly marked "Smoking area" to light up.

People generally follow rules when crossing the road, but occasionally, people do cross on red signals – especially in the city. Remember that rules are in place to keep you safe. Are you really in that much of a hurry anyway?

Chopsticks and rules at the dinner table

If there's one thing you take away, remember to never use your own chopsticks to grab food from a communal dish, unless you have the "OK" from everyone on the table. One workaround is to use the non-pointed ends to tuck in, or to serve others.

Speaking of which, it's polite to serve others before serving yourself. Passing food from one pair of chopsticks to another or sticking them upright inside bowls are BIG no-nos – this is reserved for funeral rites.

Remember that rules are in place to keep you safe. Are you really in that much of a hurry anyway?

11

Language and Phrases

Japan's language barrier is a common misconception. As all Japanese students study English for a minimum of six years in secondary school, most Japanese locals will speak at least a little English. Sometimes, you might find that people are hesitant to try their English on you, but you'll likely find that you can communicate in basic English in a huge variety of situations while traveling around Japan.

With that out of the way, it's still useful (not to mention polite), to learn a few Japanese phrases. You'll find that people are more likely to open up to you and, especially the older generation, more likely to share their fascinating stories with you.

For more useful travel phrases and an audio guide to pronunciation, don't forget to check out our World Nomads Japanese Language Guide app, available for iOS and Android.

❝❞

Japanese locals will speak at least a little English. Sometimes, you might find that people are hesitant to try their English on you.

Useful Japanese Phrases

Hello: *konnichiwa*

Thank You:
Arigatou gozaimasu or simply, (informal) *arigatou*

Excuse Me/I'm Sorry: *Sumimasen*

Please: O*negai shimas*

My Name is "X": *Watashi wa "X"*

I would like "X", please: *"X" o kudasai*

Where is the "X":
"X" wa doko desu ka? or, (informal) *doko deska?*

Do you have a room?: *Oheya aitemas ka?*

How Much?: *Ikula?*

Please say that more slowly:
Yukkuli hanashite kudasai

Those drugs aren't mine!:
Sono dolaggu watashino dewa alimasen

Goodbye: *Sayoonara*

12

Is Japan Safe?

Japan is generally safe for tourists. People on the street and on public transport will look at you with a sense of curiosity, and are some of the friendliest, warmest people you could meet. In saying this, there are some things you should know about general safety before your Japanese adventure begins.

Yakuza (gokudō) and crime in Japan

Despite popular belief, Japan is not immune from organised crime – the Japanese call their version of this organisation the **yakuza**. Known for their discipline and their widespread presence, they are not to be underestimated.

The *yakuza* are responsible for many different criminal syndicates in Japan, ranging from petty gambling and prostitution circles, to having power in the Japanese media, politics, and in the

financial sector. While they have a large presence in Japan, it should be noted that they are unlikely to harm or target tourists.

In saying this, you should still exercise the usual amount of caution that you would in your home country.

Drink-spiking in Japan

While Japan has a busy and exciting night scene, particularly in cities like Tokyo and Kyoto, there has been an increase in reported incidents of drink-spiking over the past few years.

These occurrences, in some instances, have led to theft and even physical and sexual assault of the victim. While this is usually rare, you should exercise particular caution – don't accept drinks from strangers, and don't leave drinks unattended.

Solo female travellers should be especially careful, as they can be a perfect

> **66 99**
>
> **While the yakuza have a large presence in Japan, they are unlikely to harm or target tourists.**

target for these attacks. In saying this, practicing a bit of common sense and being aware of drink-spiking dangers will go a long way.

Earthquake safety

Each year, there are around 1,500 earthquakes in Japan, so the locals are used to a few trembles. That doesn't mean you shouldn't stay alert.

A big part of staying safe is to have easy access to accurate information. A few extra seconds of warning can give you all the time you need to prepare for an earthquake. Stay connected and download a free Earthquake Early Warning app.

If you do find yourself in an earthquake, take shelter under a sturdy piece of furniture or under a doorway. If there is nowhere to hide, cover your head with something like a pillow. Don't move

If you're out in the open, crouch down on the ground and cover your head.

until the earthquake stops.

Falling debris from rooftops after an earthquake is a common cause of injury, so don't go outside. If you're out in the open, crouch down on the ground and cover your head.

LGBT travellers in Japan

Japanese society places more emphasis on group identity and values than personal expression. Sexuality — homo or hetero — is considered a private matter; it's not flaunted with public displays of affection, or discussed.

Because of this, much of local gay life is not just hidden — it's inaccessible. This is even more so for lesbians in Japan, who remain invisible.

That said, homosexuality is legal in Japan and Japanese travel providers are also starting to recognise the gay travel market.

If you know where to look, LGBTQI+ safe bars and spaces are aplenty, especially in Tokyo. So do a little homework before you go, or join a locally-guided bar crawl and meet some friendly locals to discover more about gay Japan.

Getting Around

Travelling around Japan is exciting, mysterious and awe-inspiring, but it doesn't have to be difficult or unsafe. From mastering Japan's biggest cities, to shooting through mountain ranges on the shinkansen bullet train, or sleeping toe-to-toe with Japanese families on a ferry, there are a myriad of options to get around.

Inner-city trains/metro

In Japanese cities, the rail and metro systems are often the easiest ways to travel. You can usually buy multiple-day passes, making it even more convenient. Rail staff operate at all ticket gates and are generally very helpful to foreign tourists.

Trams

Several major cities including Hiroshima, Kumamoto and Nagasaki have tram systems, which are a great way to get around. These cities often offer 1-3 day passes which allow you unlimited travel on the tram system.

Buses

Buses are available in major cities, but they aren't very easy to use for non-Japanese speakers. Typically, trains, metro, and trams are more convenient and clearly signposted.

Taxis

These are everywhere in Japan, and their distinctive look makes them easy to pick outside train stations and on the streets. However, they are by far the most expensive mode of transport in Japan, so think twice before ordering a taxi from Tokyo's Shinjuku station to Narita airport, for example, a journey which will set you back an eye-watering USD$240.

Shinkansen

One of the best ways to travel if you want to get to your destination with minimum hassle is Japan's **shinkansen**, or bullet train. Hurtling through mountains and around coastlines at up to 320kph (200mph), the *shinkansen* brings even the furthest parts of japan within an easy few hours' journey. A convenient way to travel cross-country in Japan is use the **Japan Rail**

"

Typically, trains, metro and trams are more convenient and clearly signposted.

way to travel around Japan is with a ticket called the **Seishun 18 Kippu**. This ticket is unbelievably good value for money compared to other modes of transport, giving you 5 non-consecutive days of unlimited rail travel, excluding *shinkansen* trains. It is only available at certain times of year though, so make sure to check the website to help plan your trip.

Ferry
Japan consists of thousands of islands, and you can catch ferries from many of the larger cities such as Tokyo and Osaka. Many ferries even have uniquely Japanese features like public bath houses. Overnight ferries involve sleeping in a room full of Japanese families, which is a great way to see a slice of Japanese life, but bring ear plugs in case you end up next to granddad.

Pass, which is available to those on tourist visas and gives you unlimited rail access to all but the fastest *shinkansen* for 7-21 days. It can only be bought before arriving in Japan. Be advised though — without the JR pass, *shinkansen* tickets are pricey. If speed is your priority and you don't have a rail pass, domestic flights will almost certainly be cheaper.

Night buses
These are a very low-cost option, and leave stations of metropolitan areas in the evening, arriving first thing in the morning. Taking a bus through the mountains of Japan can be a great experience — not recommended for light sleepers though!

Express trains
For those with more time on their hands, by far the most economical

Visas and Vaccinations

In the excitement of finding cheap flights and planning trips to temples and sumo matches, it's easy to forget mundane things such as checking your visa requirements or getting your shots. Here's what you need to know.

Visas for short visits

Travellers from Australia, New Zealand, the UK, US, and some European countries are covered by the Reciprocal Visa Exemption Arrangements with Japan. Holders of these passports may enter as a "Temporary Visitors", and visas are not required for a timeframe shorter than 90 days. To see if your country is covered, check the Japanese Ministry of Foreign Affairs website.

Visas for longer visits

As of the 23rd June 2015, travellers can stay for up to 12 months in Japan for tourism and recreational purposes under Japan's Longer Stays program.

The basics are that you need to be over 18, have no accompanying children, have private medical travel insurance, and a certain amount of savings to sustain your trip. Check with your local Japanese embassy for more specifics.

Working visas

If you plan on working in Japan, this requires a different type of visa altogether. As there are 27 different types of visas issued by Japan, it's impossible to list all of these requirements here.

Be aware, however, that Japanese working visas are only issued to applicants with a high level of knowledge in skilled professions. For specific details, get in touch with your closest Japanese embassy.

Vaccinations

There are no vaccines required to visit Japan. However, it's always a good idea to take some basic health precautions before traveling.

The US Centre for Disease Control (CDC) recommends that travellers should be up to date on routine vaccines before your trip. These include measles-mumps-rubella (MMR) vaccine, diphtheria-tetanus-pertussis vaccine, varicella (chickenpox) vaccine, polio vaccine, and your yearly flu shot.

> "There are no vaccines required to visit Japan. However, it's always a good idea to take some basic health precautions."

TOKYO

As well as being Japan's capital and the world's most densely-populated city, Tokyo is famous for combining the charms of tradition and the buzz of the modern world. Explore millennia-old Shinto shrines and village-like lanes, then hop on the metro and arrive at the flashing neon lights of dizzying skyscrapers, filled with world-class shopping and Michelin-starred restaurants. Get ready to be swept up by this buzzing metropolis.

18

Must See and Do

Although the palace itself remains closed for most of the year, it opens its gates to the public during the Emperor's New Year's speech.

North-East Tokyo

Visit **Sensoji**, Tokyo's oldest temple. On the way there, stop off at the food stalls to grab a treat and buy some handmade *maneki neko* (good luck charms).

North-East Tokyo is famous for its **sumo schools**, which regularly hold sumo-wrestling tournaments. If you're visiting during the off-season, you might still be able to catch one of the practice matches.

The **Edo Tokyo Museum**, which exhibits life in Tokyo both past and present, is another must-see in the area.

Central Tokyo

In the heart of Tokyo lies the **Imperial Palace**, surrounded by the high-rises of Tokyo's business districts. Although the palace itself remains closed for most of the year, it opens its gates to the public during the Emperor's New Year's speech, and in autumn to view the season's changing colours.

Don't miss **Ginza**, a bustling commercial district with many brand stores and, more importantly, the **Kabuki-za theatre**. Kabuki, a classical, stylised form of drama, is only performed in select theatres, and is especially cherished in cities outside Kyoto.

West Tokyo

In western Tokyo, **Harajuku** draws thousands of visitors every day. After all, it's the hotspot for J-Pop, and fashion, and also the home of **Meiji Jingu**, Tokyo's most important shrine.

Shinjuku, to the north of Harajuku, is the more affordable rival of Ginza. It's a favourite shopping district for locals. Here, you'll will find the narrow alley, known as **Golden Gai**, which is famous for its small restaurants and pubs with excellent food. For an unforgettable night out, **Roppongi** is packed with clubs – and people – or **Ni-Chome**, Tokyo's queer-friendly district, are definitely the places to go.

Southern Tokyo

For anime and robot enthusiasts, the **Odaiba district**, with its full-scale Gundam statue, is a must-visit. Make sure you take a seflie in front of the mechanical giant!

The fresh seafood of **Tsukiji Fish Market** has been the dream destination of chefs and foodies alike. Local restaurants often go at the break of dawn to get the freshest seafood for their customers. Be sure to find a sushi shop around here for some of the freshest sashimi in town.

Outdoor Activities

Shinjuku Gyoen

This lush, 144-acre park and garden sits smack in the middle of the city, offering locals a respite from the surrounding skyscrapers. Known for its beauty during cherry blossom season, the park is a splendid and convenient place for a picnic or stroll.

Tokyo by bike

There are some set cycling courses in places like **Yoyogi Park** or the **Imperial Palace**, but it's also a treat to just get lost and explore the alleys and backstreets of random neighbourhoods.

You're sure to turn up some gems like small temples, neighbourhood bars, and old shopping streets. There are many places to rent a bicycle. Just beware not to ride by yourself after dark.

Urban hot springs at Ooedo Onsen Monogatari

Even in Tokyo, you can experience Japanese-style communal bathing in places like **Ooedo Onsen Monogatari**, a large hot spring spa complex decorated to look like the Edo-era capital.

Don a cotton *yukata*, dip your toes in the steaming footbaths, or take it all off for a relaxing soak in the open-air pools. Note that, as in most hot springs in Japan, tattoos are not permitted.

It's a treat to just get lost and explore the alleys and backstreets.

Hiking Mt. Mitake and Mt. Takao

At the western of edge of Tokyo, still within the city limits in the Tama region, are **Mt. Mitake** and **Mt. Takao**, two popular spots for people who want to get in some more serious hiking.

Both can be reached by train from central Tokyo in about an hour or so. From here you can hike or take a cable car up the mountain. You'll find more walking trails, ancient shrines and temples, beautiful flora and fauna, and stunning views of both Tokyo city and distant **Mt. Fuji**.

Diving Ogasawara

The **Ogasawara Islands** lay a thousand miles south of Tokyo, yet it's still considered part of the Tokyo Metropolitan Area.

These far-flung islands offer excellent diving and snorkelling among the tropical fish and coral reefs that ring the islands.

There are more than 30 islands to choose from, which can be reached by ferry to the main island of **Chichijima**, or "Father Island."

20

Nightlife

Izakayas

Izakayas can be found in every suburb, and are great venues to connect with locals. Try **Zakoya** in **Shimokitazawa** for a cosy, traditional interior, delicious food and great sake selection.

Late-night cafes

In the grungy Tokyo suburb of **Shimokitazawa**, you'll find a number of small bohemian bars, vintage shops, cafes and restaurants, open late along pedestrian-only streets.

Just a few blocks from the izakaya **Zakoya** is **Café Propaganda**. Open until sunrise on weekends, this laid-back lounge offers large shisha pipes, giant antique couches, delicious food and unique cocktails at any hour.

Yakitori and street food

One of Japan's most deliciously famous street food is *yakitori* (grilled chicken skewers). A fantastic area to get a feel for this style of eating is Shinjuku's **Omoide Yokocho**. The narrow alleyways are lined with lanterns, bar stools and grills offering authentic local cuisine, and *yakitori* as the main event.

A couple of blocks away is the boozier version of Omoide Yokocho, in the famous **Golden Gai**. Golden Gai's watering holes are found in small alleys, often only seating 8 or so people.

Nomihodais and karaoke

One way to drink on the cheap in Tokyo is *nomihodai*, Japanese for 'all you can drink'. Most late-night karaoke

> " "
> **The narrow alleyways are lined with lanterns, bar stools and grills offering authentic local cuisine.**

venues offer *nomihodai*. For those who believe there is nothing better than the combination of unlimited alcohol, cheesy video clips, and horrible singing – this place is for you.

If karaoke isn't your thing, try **Bar Mist** in **Roppongi**, which features three hours of all-you-can-drink for only ¥1,000.

Pecha Kucha

For those of you who don't know, Pecha Kucha is a series of 20-slide image presentations, with each slide only appearing for 20 seconds. This monthly hub of creatives, designers, thinkers and basically anyone with something to say, has become a must-see at Roppongi's self-proclaimed gallery/lounge/bar/club/ creative kitchen **SuperDeluxe**.

Bizarre themed restaurants and shows

Two must-visit entertainment restaurants for the ultimate bizarre Tokyo experience are Harajuku's **Kawaii Monster Café**, and Shinjuku's **Robot Restaurant**. Both feature crazy entertainment, music, shows, food, and drinks.

One-Day Itinerary

Street food, lucky charms and Sensoji Temple

First stop, **Asakusa!** The district is Tokyo's oldest remaining entertainment area with an Edo-period charm. At the heart of the district lies **Sensoji Temple**, Tokyo's oldest temple, devoted to the goddess *Kannon*. **Nakamise street** leading up to Sensoji is lined with countless small shops, selling a variety of small items and street food. These make for great souvenirs.

Experience Edo culture at Ueno Park

By taking the Ginza Line from Asakusa to Ueno Station, we arrive at **Ueno Park**. One of Tokyo's most popular parks to view cherry blossoms in spring, it's also home to a number of temples and shrines.

The most famous spot here is the **Tokyo National Museum**, which features national treasures and cultural heritage items. If you're interested in museums, **Edo Tokyo Museum** only takes 25min on the Oedo Line from **Ueno-okachimachi** to Ryogoku Station.

Ryogoku Kokugikan is also located near the station, and if you happen to be in Tokyo at the right time, you could even catch the **sumo-wrestling** tournament when it's held in the city.

Explore Ginza, the beating heart of Tokyo

Heading to central Tokyo from Ueno on the JR Yamanote Line brings us to Tokyo Station, tucked in between **Marunouchi** and **Ginza**. The building itself is one of the city's most important symbols, as well as a historic reminder of Japan's modernisation at the brink of the 20th century.

While Marunouchi is a business district, Ginza is commercial, known for its brand stores and **Kabuki-za**, where you can enjoy a kabuki performance.

Stroll through the Imperial Palace Gardens

The wide road in front of Tokyo station connects it with the **Imperial Palace**. While you cannot visit the palace itself, its **East Gardens** are open to the public and well worth a tour.

Cosplay in Harajuku

The Chiyoda Line gets us from Otemachi Station on the northern side

> ❝❞
> **Harajuku is known throughout the world as the centre of teenage J-Pop and extravagant fashion.**

of the East Gardens to **Meiji-jingu Mae**, near the popular **Harajuku** district. Harajuku is known throughout the world as the centre of teenage J-Pop and extravagant fashion. **Takeshita Street**, in particular, is lined with many small shops, cafes, and boutiques.

Pray for good fortune at Meiji Jingu Shrine

Another not-to-be-missed sight in **Harajuku** is **Meiji Jingu Shrine**, Tokyo's most important shrine. Meiji Jingu is dedicated to Emperor Meiji's soul and that of his wife.

Take a stroll through the forests of **Yoyogi Park** surrounding the shrine and the **Tokyo Metropolitan Government Building**. The observatories on the top floor of each tower offers a stunning view over Tokyo's skyline and, on a clear afternoon, you might even spot **Mt Fuji** in the distance.

Sample Tokyo's world-famous cuisine in Shinjuku

Cap off your day by walking east towards **Shinjuku** for an evening of shopping – we recommend checking out all the latest tech gadgets!

Before you leave Tokyo, don't miss out on the city's world-famous dining scene with a delicious dinner in a small restaurant or pub in **Golden Gai**.

Getting around

Rail and metro
The most convenient way to get around. Get a multiple day pass to save money, and download an offline, English version of the metro map to help you navigate your journey.

Buses
Buses are available throughout Tokyo, but are not easy to use for non-Japanese speakers.

Taxis
The most expensive mode of transport. Think twice before ordering a taxi from Shinjuku station to Narita airport, which will cost USD$240.

Ferries
Used to get to the man-made islands of Tokyo Bay, or travelling between destinations near water.

TOKYO

This huge, wealthy and fascinating metropolis brings high-tech visions of the future side-by-side with glimpses of old Japan, and has something for everyone.

HIGHLIGHTS

Asakusa and Senso-ji Temple

An old, traditional feel.

Hanami flower viewing

The blossoms come out in late March.

Mt. Fuji

Japan's iconic, tallest mountain.

The Imperial Palace

The official residence of the Japanese Imperial Family since 1868.

ASAKUSA AND SENSO-JI TEMPLE

Asakusa has an old, traditional feel with the Senso-ji Temple, the famous Kaminari-mon Gate, and the over 200-metre long Nakamise Street.

HANAMI FLOWER VIEWING

Set up with food, drinks and music under the trees to enjoy hanami, or flower viewing. The blossoms come out in late March in Tokyo and only last for two weeks.

MT. FUJI

It's an easy one or two-days trip from Tokyo to Mount Fuji, Japan's iconic, tallest mountain. The best places for viewing from a distance are Hakone or in the vicinity of Fuji Five Lakes.

THE IMPERIAL PALACE

Tokyo's Imperial Palace is located in the Chiyoda Ward in the centre of the city. The Palace has been the official residence of the Japanese Imperial Family since 1868. It is surrounded by a series of moats and high walls within extensive and impeccably maintained gardens.

TOKYO SKYTREE

Take a trip to one of the two observation decks at Tokyo Skytree for incredible views of the city. At 634 metres high, this is the world's tallest, free-standing telecommunications tower.

TOKYO
ACCOMODATION

*Based on 482 reviews

RYOKAN SAWANOYA

2-3-11 Yanaka,
Taito, Tokyo Prefecture, 110-0001
Tel:

Review by TripAdvisor Traveller petehob
Reviewed 28/12/2016

This is a beautifully kept and very friendly Ryokan, close to the rail sta-tion, but nice a quiet.

We took two bedrooms and our chil-dren loved staying here. The owner is a sweet fellow and when I asked him to sign his book one evening he told me: "Tomorrow morning I sign. Tonight I have been in neighbourhood with friends and now cannot write."

*Based on 748 reviews

FAMILY INN SAIKO

2-34-16 Nagasaki,
Toshima, Tokyo Prefecture, 171-0051
Tel:

Review by TripAdvisor Traveller Raymund T
Reviewed 31/12/2016

Just returned from a 2 week family vacation to
Japan(1st timers) & spent our 1st 5 nights there. Wanted to experience a traditional Ryokan before moving on to a 5 star type of accommodation. Have to admit it was as good if not better than the more " glitzy" hotels we stayed at. Reasons? 1). After spending all day in the crowds of Tokyo it was a nice change of pace to walk through the streets of Shi-inamachi & experience the quietness of the lo...

TOKYO

ACCOMODATION

*Based on 30 reviews

PALACE HOTEL TOKYO

1-1-1 Marunouchi,
Chiyoda, Tokyo Prefecture, 100-0005 Tel:
+81345402211

Review by TripAdvisor Traveller
TravelWorldWisely
Reviewed 7/01/2017

Once you've done them all: Park Hyatt,
Grand Hyatt, Peninsula, Mandarin,
and may be even the Aman, chances are,
you'll come back here. Because it's the
most Japanese of them all. Because the
service is impeccable
(and do splurge on the Club level room and
the 19th floor lounge will become your
retreat from the hustle of the big hotel).
Because the quality of restaurants makes
you feel bad you go out. Because they
remember you here. Because the vi...

*Based on 916 reviews

MANDARIN ORIENTAL, TOKYO

2-1-1 Nihonbashi Muromachi , Chuo,
Tokyo Prefecture, 103-8328
Tel: +81332708800

Review by TripAdvisor Traveller
David_in_Melbourne
Reviewed 6/01/2017

I've stayed at a lot of hotels ... this property
stands above most for its utter all-round
excellence.

Our checkin experience was as smooth as
could be expected, in spite of our booking
(via TA) providing incorrect details to the
property. Reception is located on Level 38
- right at the top of the property, and it has
outstanding
views over Tokyo ,.., it's hard not to be
somewhat distracted during checkin! Our
room, on L35 enjoyed some great vi.,,

TOKYO
WINE & DINE

*Based on 59 reviews

MAIDREAMIN AKIHABARA
THE THIRD STORE
4-4-2 Sotokanda, Kyoei-sotokanda-daii-chi
BLDG.4FChiyoda, 101-0021
Tel: +81 3-6206-8180

Review by TripAdvisor Traveller smoov3
Reviewed 7/01/2017

The maids will make you feel at home, I recommend the kawaii combo and the pork cutlet in curry sauce. It's an excellent break from the cold if visiting akiharaba in the winter.

*Based on 57 reviews

TAPAS MOLECULAR BAR

2-1-1 Nihonbashi Muromachi, 38F, Manda-rin Oriental TokyoChuo, 103-8328
Tel: +81 3-3270-8188

Review by TripAdvisor Traveller
Vegemitelover
Reviewed 31/12/2016

We visited the restaurant one lunchtime. The restaurant has been recommended by others as one to visit in Japan. It was one of the earlier restaurants specialising in molecules cuisine in Asia.

The meal was served at the bar. There were only five guests and the key chef serving us was Ping. The meal was served over a two hour period which for sixteen dishes was quite fast.

TOKYO
WINE & DINE

👀 ⭕⭕⭕⭕⭕ *Based on 9 38   reviews

HAKUSHU

17-10 Sakuragaokacho, 1F MCD Bldg.
Shibuya, Tokyo Prefecture, 150-0031
Tel: +81 3-3461-0546

Review by TripAdvisor Traveller
kimtyhappy
Reviewed 8/01/2017

We open tripadvisor for here when i stay in shibuya and walk to this place. Waiting about 2 hr for 3 people and we order the best order in here.Beef is very Delicious and service is 5 star same big restaurants.We get more for 1 Piece and this is place that i cannot forget all of my life :D we will come back next year for sure.

👀 ⭕⭕⭕⭕⭕ *Based on 7 24   reviews

T'S TANTAN TOKYOSTATION
1-9-1 Marunouchi, Keiyo Street
Chiyoda, Tokyo Prefecture, Tel:
+81 3-3218-8040

Review by TripAdvisor Traveller
Taha A
Reviewed 4/01/2017

Had the veggie ramen. It was absolute-ly epic Lu delicious. The little pieces of veggie meat tasted almost like beef.
I don't eat pork so this was a great option to try ramen here in Tokyo. You have to go in the Station past the ticket checkpoint to get to it.

KYOTO

Located at the central part of Honshuu island, Kyoto was the former capital of Japan for over a thousand years. Today, it still retains much of its old-world charm. Over the centuries, the city was destroyed by many wars and fires, but countless temples, shrines, zen gardens and other historic landmarks still remain. It's also home to many of Japan's most important matsuris and serves as the training ground of Geishas, an integral part of the city's thriving nightlife. With so much to see, do, and eat, you won't want to rush your stay here.

Must See and Do

Sanjusangendo

Laying slightly off-the-beaten-path, **Sanjusangendo** is located east of Kyoto Station. Founded in 1164, this temple is famous for its 1001 statues of the goddess of mercy, *Kannon*, in the 120m wooden hall. The name literally translates to "33 intervals", the traditional method of measuring the size of a building and definitely an impressive sight to behold.

Kyoto International Manga Museum

More of a library, the manga museum features a collection of over 300,000 manga that you can read at your leisure. Don't worry if you can't read Japanese – about 1,000 of these are in English.

Ryoanji

Famous for its gravel-and-rock Zen garden, **Ryoanji** is generally regarded as the finest expression of Zen. As you're seated on the deck of the head priest's former residence, you won't be able to see all 15 stones in the garden. There's a lesson there somewhere!

Nanzenji

Nanzenji is the head temple of one of the schools within the Rinzai sector of Japanese Zen Buddhism, and includes an impressive network of interconnected sub-temples. Its spacious grounds and ancient wooden

architecture is one-of-a-kind. In autumn, the grounds are especially rewarding as the surrounding forests change colours, transforming the scenery.

Arashiyama

Located on the western outskirt of Kyoto, this is a popular destination to enjoy nature and the soothing air flowing over the river. Its famous **bamboo grove** lets you wander in a mystical forest, through which you won't even see the sky.

Nijo Castle

Only a few hundred meters away from Kyoto's **Imperial Palace, Nijo Castle** was built as a symbol of power for the shogunate – feudal Japan's last military government. With floors that squeak when you step on them (called "nightingale" floors), and hidden

> **Located on the western outskirt of Kyoto, Arashiyama is a popular destination to enjoy nature and the soothing air flowing over the river.**

guards stationed throughout, the castle was designed to impress anyone who would come for an audience.

Ginkakuji

Known as "The Temple of the Silver Pavilion", **Ginkakuji** was so named because the moonlight reflecting on the building's dark exterior was said to give it a silvery appearance. Take in the serenity of the moss garden and enjoy the zen of the grounds as you walk along its famous circular route.

Kinkakuji

The pavilion used to be part of a vast retirement residence for shogun Yoshimitsu, but it was converted to a Zen temple after his death. The pavilion's top two floors are completely covered in gold leaf and perched on the edge of a large pond. It's a sight to behold.

Kiyomizu-dera

The "Temple of Pure Water" is a popular sight throughout the year, as visitors are drawn in by its impressive architecture. **Kiromizu-dera** is best known for its wooden stage, built in 780 and made entirely without nails. We definitely recommend checking out it's stunning views over Kyoto during Cherry Blossom Festival or late autumn, as it's the perfect spot to take in (and photograph) the hundreds of cherry and maple trees in the valley below.

Fushimi Inari Taisha

Voted as Kyoto's #1 attraction, **Fushimi Inari Taisha**'s visitors make their way through its vermilion *torii* gates towards the sacred **Mt. Inari**, which is dedicated to the Shinto god of rice. Foxes are said to be *Inari's* messengers, which explains the many fox statues watching over visitors throughout the grounds.

Its tranquillity, charm, and above all, beauty, make it hard for anyone to deny its sheer attractiveness.

> **"**
> We definitely recommend checking out Kiyomizu-dera's stunning views over Kyoto during Cherry Blossom Festival.

Outdoor Activities

Arashiyama

There are numerous walking and hiking paths around **Arashiyama**, which are liberally sprinkled with temples and traditional gardens, such as **Tenryuji, Gioji,** and **Katsura Rikyu**. Make sure you visit the monkey park and mingle (and take selfies) with free-roaming Japanese macaques.

Maruyama Park

Head over to **Maruyama** for a stroll through the classical garden, with paths that wind around ponds reflecting the greenery. In the spring, this is an extremely popular spot to do *hanami*, or cherry blossom viewing.

Philosopher's Walk

The narrow stone path from **Ginkakuji** to **Eikando** is called *Tetsugaku no michi*, or **Philosopher's Walk**.

The pedestrian path runs under a procession of cherry trees, along a canal. In addition to the major temples, the path is lined with smaller shrines and temples, a few small cafes, and shops offering both traditional and modern art.

Kuramadera and Mt. Kurama

Kurama Temple sits in the foothills of **Mt. Kurama** in northern Kyoto. The area is said to be home to many spirits, such as the mythological *tengu* (long-nosed goblins), and the healing art of *reiki* is said to have been born here.

It's possible to hike up or take a tram

“A regular bicycle can be rented for as little as ¥500 per day.

part of the way. There are also natural hot springs in the area that allow day access or overnight stays.

Higashiyama by bicycle

Higashiyama is a district with plenty to see, and is especially pleasant by bicycle. Highlights in the area include the famous temples **Kiyomizudera** and **Kodaiji,** and **Yasaka Shrine**. The narrow streets between them are stuffed with traditional shops and buildings.

A regular bicycle can be rented for as little as ¥500 per day, and if you want an electric bike (to help you with some of the hills in this district), those go for around ¥2,000.

Sanzenin and Ohara by bicycle

For a more ambitious cycling trip, head up to the village of **Ohara**. The ride is about 20km with some uphill climbs, and should take a couple of hours.

Once there, explore the temple complex of **Sanzein,** and the pretty **Otonoashi Waterfall**. There are hot spring inns in the area too if you wish to stay overnight.

Nightlife

Bars and clubs

If you're looking for a more relaxed evening, **Pig and Whistle** is the place to go. This British pub has a good selection of drinks and food, and it's a friendly place to meet locals and other international travellers!

You'll be welcomed with a free drink on arrival when you step inside **Kitsune nightclub**. Filled with glowsticks and wacky Japanese entertainment, you're in for a crazy night. The club is open every day of the week, including Sunday nights.

For a more chilled out vibe, head to **Jittoku**, located in an old sake brewery. The Japanese call Jittoku a live-house; featuring many live music acts ranging from rock, blues, Japanese pop, Irish fiddle, electronica, and more.

Places to eat

Kyoto is home to many cheap and delicious sushi trains. **Kappa Sushi** offers a wide variety and great prices, but for authentic handmade sushi, **Musashi Sushi** is a great spot to eat. There are hundreds of cheap sushi trains to explore, so don't be afraid to try as many as possible.

Menbakaichidai Fire Ramen Restaurant in Kyoto is a great experience; the local staff are welcoming, and encourage tourists to come into their restaurant as you walk by. Dinner hours can get busy for them, so it's best to avoid the 6pm-8pm rush.

> ❝❞
> **Pontocho is a narrow alley packed with restaurants, with a wide range of options for dining, including traditional Kyoto cuisine.**

Pontocho is a narrow alley packed with restaurants, with a wide range of options for dining, including traditional Kyoto cuisine. The atmosphere of this area is worth checking out whether you are looking for a proper meal or just a place to relax and have a drink.

Entertainment

There are plenty of market-style stores and food venues to choose from at **Shinkyogoku shopping arcade**. You could spend hours exploring this area if this is your thing.

Gear Kyoto is a non-verbal performance, so that both locals and international visitors can enjoy the show. The show involves magic, dance, comedy, and mime. If you're interested in theatre and have a spare night in Kyoto, it's definitely worth checking out.

Round 1 is a multi-story amusement centre. You can rent a private karaoke booth, enjoy hours of bowling, play arcade games, hop into a photo booth, and check out Las Vegas style gambling. Even if you're not interested in doing any of these things, it's worth visiting the venue just to check it out.

One-Day Itinerary

Early morning at Kiyomizu-dera

The uphill path to **Kiyomizu-dera** gets congested as the day goes on, but the temple opens at 6am. This is the perfect time to enjoy a quiet morning stroll around the temple, and down to the **Otowa waterfall**. Take a moment to drink its magical waters for luck in love, studies, or for a long life.

After your visit to the temple, spend your walk back down sampling snacks at souvenir shops. We recommend the various flavours of *Yatsuhashi*, a triangle-shaped mochi.

Near Kiyomizu-dera is your next stop, **Sanjusangen-do**. This Buddhist temple, built in 1164, houses 1001 statues of the goddess of mercy, *Kannon*. Its name literally means "33 intervals", a traditional method of measuring the size of a building.

Built without a single nail, this old wooden temple has a stunning view that is especially magical in autumn.

Afternoon temple break, Kyoto International Manga Museum, and Nijo Castle

Call ahead and make lunch reservations at the **Samurai Cafe and Bar** near the **International Manga Museum**. Their popularity makes going in on a whim difficult.

After lunch, learn about manga at the International Manga Museum. Peruse manga translated from all over the world and get a portrait done by one of their staff artists. Depending on the day and time, you can also watch manga artists at work.

A short bike ride away from the manga museum is **Nijo Castle**. Ditch your shoes and walk on the old wooden nightingale floors at **Ninomaru Palace**. As you walk around looking at painted sliding doors, the floorboards sing. It sounds like the ancient palace is alive, with the

❝❞
Most temples stop letting visitors in 30 min before closing, so keep an eye on the clock. If you manage to time it right, the end of the day can be the best time to visit.

plucking of a thousand eerie strings. Nijo Castle also includes gardens and defensive keeps.

Late afternoon at Kinkaku-ji

If you're hungry, stop by **Ryoan-ji** for some *Yudofu* (boiled tofu). You'll have a beautiful view of the temple and its gardens during this traditional meal.

Most temples stop letting visitors in 30 min before closing, so keep an eye on the clock. If you manage to time it right, the end of the day can be the best time to visit. The doors will shut behind you, giving you enough time to take pictures at your leisure. **Kinkaku-ji**, the Golden Temple, looks absolutely

stunning as the sun starts to lower in the sky.

An evening at Arashiyama

After **Kinkaku-ji**, take a train, bus, or bike ride to **Arashiyama's bamboo grove**. There's a ton to do here and the tall bamboo grove is lit up at night.

Hidden away in the grove is **Nonomiya Shrine**. This small shrine is mentioned in *The Tale of Genji*, a classic work of Japanese literature written in the early years of the 11th century. You can also head over to **Kameyama-koen Park** to spot some monkeys, or finish your trip to Kyoto with a walk through the ethereal **Kimono Forest**.

> 66 99
> **The Golden Temple looks stunning as the sun starts to lower in the sky.**

Getting around

Rail and metro

Like Tokyo, the rail and metro systems are the easiest ways to get around. Buy multiple-day passes for convenience and save. Rail staff operate at all ticket gates and are generally very helpful to foreigners.

Buses

These aren't the most user-friendly for non-Japanese speakers, but it does cover a large part of the city.

Taxis

By far the most expensive mode of transport in Japan. Think twice before hopping in!

KYOTO

Kyoto, the former capital of Japan, embodies Japanese tradition with hundreds of Buddhist temples, Shinto shrines, zen gardens, tea houses, pagodas, and palaces.

HIGHLIGHTS

Festivals
Home to many festivals including some of Japan's biggest.

Fushimi Inari Shrine
Don't miss the hundreds of red gates.

Gion
The most famous geisha district in Japan.

Kiyomizu Temple
One of 17 World Heritage Sites listed in Kyoto by UNESCO.

FESTIVALS

Kyoto is home to many festivals including some of Japan's biggest. Gion Matsuri in July is the liveliest with other famous festivals including Aoi Matsui, Kurama no Hi-Matsuri, Jidai Matsuri, Daimonji Gozan Okuribi, and Mifune Matsuri.

FUSHIMI INARI SHRINE

Immortalised in the film Memoires of a Geisha, don't miss the hundreds of red gates at the Fushimi Inari Shrine.

GION

The most famous geisha district in Japan, Gion is a beautifully preserved collection of wooden teahouses and exclusive restaurants.

KIYOMIZU TEMPLE

Kiyomizu Temple is just one of 17 World Heritage Sites listed in Kyoto by UNESCO in 1994.

KYOTO
ACCOMODATION

*Based on 94 reviews

SHIRAUME

Shirakawa-hotori, Shinbashi-dori, Gion-machi, Higashiyama-ku, Kyoto,
Tel:

Review by TripAdvisor Traveller
christina_villarreal
Reviewed 8/01/2017

This ryokan, located on a beautiful, traditional street in Kyoto yet just steps away from prime shopping and dining areas has got to be the best service we have EVER experienced. My husband and I have stayed in 5 star/top rated hotels both large and small, as well
as luxury bed and breakfasts all over the world and THIS PLACE IS THE SUPREME of hospitality!!! The hotel's primary hostess along with the rest of the staff are all impeccable, thought...

*Based on 646 reviews

HOTEL MUME

261 Shinmonzen dori, Umemotocho, Higashiyama-ku, Kyoto, 605-0064 Tel:

Review by TripAdvisor Traveller wobbs1
Reviewed 8/01/2017

We were able to return to Kyoto and Hotel Mume this November, and were happy to find that all the good things we cited in our previous review are still true.

We reserved close to a year in advance and still didn't get our preferred room ... but that didn't matter. All the rooms we've seen are adequate. Moreover, the reason you want to stay at this hotel is the friendliness and helpfulness of the staff. Hisako and her crew make arrangements fo...

KYOTO
ACCOMODATION

*Based on 377 reviews

THE RITZ-CARLTON, KYOTO

Kamogawa Nijo-Ohashi Hotori, Nak-agyo-ku, Nakagyo-kuKyoto, 604-0902 Tel: +81757465555

Review by TripAdvisor Traveller
catrina_tang
Reviewed 5/01/2017

The entire staff at the Ritz Carlton Kyo-to far exceeded our expectations! Spe-cial thanks to Aquana for the excellent art tour and bike Kyoto activity. Thank you also for arranging to transport our passport from Tokyo to Kyoto via local courier. We appreciate the front desk staff very much!

We had a fabulous experience and looking forward to a return trip.

*Based on 219 reviews

ARASHIYAMA BENKEI

34 Sagatenryuji Susukinobabacho Ukyo-ku, Kyoto, Kyoto Prefecture, 616-8385 Tel: +81345409875

Review by TripAdvisor Traveller
robi_bg79
Reviewed 4/01/2017

Far from the noisy city center, this tra-ditional ryokan represents a real tradi-tional esperience with all the confort of modern time. The staff is very gentle and kind, the quality of the service (in-clusive meals) is superior. Spring bath area is quite small, but still adequately sized for the limited number of guests supposed to be hosted

KYOTO
WINE & DINE

Based on 106 reviews

OKONOMIYAKI KATSU

1-4 Ryoanji Saigucho, Ukyo-ku,
Kyoto, Kyoto Prefecture, 616-8011
Tel: +81 75-464-8981

Review by TripAdvisor Traveller bunodid
Reviewed 3/01/2017

Food was very good and cheap.
The couple who own the restaurant is
extremely welcoming. I definitely
recommend the place. "Feel at home"
atmosphere.

Based on 25 reviews

ARASH'S KITCHEN

16 Shogoin Sannocho, Sakyo-ku, 2F Sun Plaza,
Kyoto, Kyoto Prefecture, 606-8392 Tel: +81
80-5366-5573

Review by TripAdvisor Traveller tsara1
Reviewed 6/01/2017

To start with, the flavours, spices and
taste are just amazing here. Having
travelled Japan a fair bit I tend to get
tired of the typical Japanese, Italian and
American foods. Arash's Kitchen was a
lovely change of pace to the typical foods
you tend to find in busy cities of Japan.
The food was amazing and I've had plenty
of Arabian and Indian food in my life. Not
to mention the friendly and hilarious staff
who make your stay so much better
than ...

KYOTO
WINE & DINE

*Based on 334 reviews

SHISHIN SAMURAI
CAFE & BAR & RESTAURANT
230-1 Kamimyoukakujicho, Koromono-
tanadori Oshikoji-agaru,Kyoto, 604-0025
Tel: +81 75-231-5155

Review by TripAdvisor Traveller Emma R
Reviewed 6/01/2017

Most restaurants in Kyoto are closed over
New Years until the 4th so we were very
excited to be able to book this place for
dinner (would definitely recommend
making a reservation as the place is on the
smaller size).

The food was amazing and we ended up
ordering more than expected. The wine
was amazing and would definitely
recommend getting a bottle despite the
price. We chose to order off the menu
rather than get a set menu. The samurai
burg...

*Based on 336 reviews

OTSUKA

20-10 Sagatenryuji Setogawacho, Ukyo-ku,
Kyoto, Kyoto Prefecture, 616-8376 Tel: +81
75-864-7989

Review by TripAdvisor Traveller Natek3232
Reviewed 7/01/2017

Went here after walking through the
bamboo groves. We were excited because
of the great reviews and there also was not
a long wait to get a seat.

We tired one order of the A4 Wagyu and
one order of the A5 Wagyu. When we went
here we thought it was great. The A4 was
less fatty and more to my preference.
However a few days later we went to Kobe
and had much thicker pieces of beef that
were much more special tasting than this.
Looking back it was g...

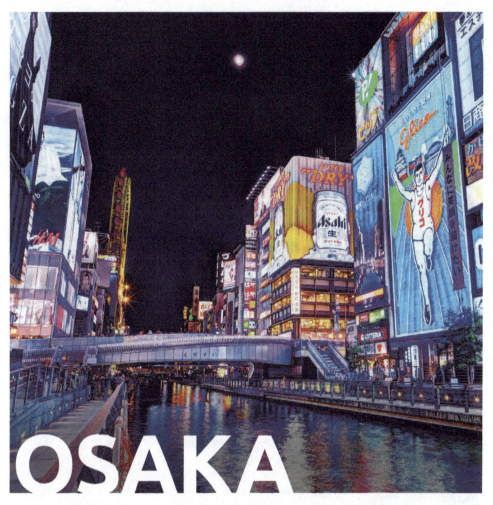

OSAKA

Despite being Japan's second-largest city, Osaka is far too often overlooked by travellers. But don't worry, we won't let you make the same mistake. With some of the country's most fun-loving people and a world-class drinking and dining culture, it's a perennial favourite among locals and foodies the world over. It is, after all, known as the "nation's kitchen" and boasts of being the birthplace of okonomiyaki, takoyaki, and udon. So do as the locals and grab a bike – plus a pair of chopsticks – and join us in exploring this food-lover's paradise.

Must See and Do

Shinsekai

Considered one of the dodgiest areas in Osaka, **Shinsekai** has a lot of character – and characters! Visit at night and choose a *kushi-katsu* restaurant. We suggest a smaller one with plastic chairs outside (in summer) to best enjoy the view of **Tsutenkaku Tower**, a 100m, octagonal construction modelled after the Eiffel Tower. Get set ordering deep-fried foods on sticks and you're in for a top night.

We recommend plum and shiso chicken, but go crazy and try cheese-cake, or half-boiled egg. Prices are usually between ¥80 to ¥100 per stick, and up to ¥500 for a beer – which *kushi-katsu* goes really well with. Don't forget to yell *okini!* (oh-kee-nee "thank you") as you leave.

Dotonbori

Another sweet night spot is **Dotonbori**. See the famous **Glico man**, and the **robot crab**, revel in the

neon glare from karaoke bar signs, and the run-down, 1980's cyberpunk atmosphere.

Turn down a few lanes off the main drag to the quiet, cobble-stoned street of restaurants – which the crowds never seem to find. For travellers who prefer people-watching, find a spot on **Dotonboribashi bridge** among spiky-haired hosts plying their trade. Beware of the optimistic high school girls attempting to ride their bicycles through the crowd.

Osaka Castle

Osaka castle is incredibly impressive. Outside the 30m high castle walls, the beautiful park is a favourite spot during cherry blossom season for BBQs.

The main building itself is a reconstruction, with a museum inside. Some dislike the elevator, however it

> **"**
> Turn down a few lanes off the main drag to the quiet, cobble-stoned street of restaurants – which the crowds never seem to find.

46

temples and shrines as Kyoto, but it is the site of the oldest Buddhist temple in Japan, **Shitennoji**.

From the pagoda, the other temple buildings, beautiful rows of hanging lanterns, to the pond of abandoned pet turtles – there's plenty to see here.

On the 21st and 22nd of every month, there is also a huge flea market. If you're willing to venture out on the 11th of February, you will witness **Doya Doya Matsuri**, a sympathetic-shudder-inducing festival, where high school boys run through sheets of freezing water to catch paper charms, and ensure their luck for the year to come.

does increase the ease of access for travellers with walking difficulties.

Tobita Shinchi

Less family-friendly, but interesting on many levels, is the neighbourhood of **Tobita Shinchi**. This large brothel district remains true to a traditional style that has otherwise vanished from Japan.

Beautifully dressed prostitutes sit in the doorways, waiting for customers. Even in winter, they sit by kerosene heaters, ensconced in fluffy blankets that still manage to reveal some skin.

Black SUVs idle along the street, reminding nervous tourists that Osaka's underbelly is watching, unless they are otherwise engaged. Photography is strictly not allowed.

Shitennoji

Osaka is not as well known for its

" "

Black SUVs idle along the street, reminding nervous tourists that Osaka's underbelly is watching.

Outdoor Activities

Picnic among the cherry blossoms at Tennoji Park

Tennoji Park is a world away from the hustle and bustle of the city. Situated in the southern part of the city, the park is a botanical oasis, right next to Tennoji Station. Pack yourself a picnic and take some time to enjoy its natural beauty. It's the perfect spot for bike riding, or a leisurely afternoon stroll.

The best time to visit is in spring, when the native *sakura* (cherry blossom) are in full bloom. You'll be spoilt for choice on statues, open spaces for sport, cafés, and restaurants.

Take photos around scenic Minoo Park

If the inner-city escape of **Tennoji Park** wasn't enough for you, head further north to the splendour of **Minoo** (Minoh) **Park**. It's most well-known for the walking trail, **Takimichi**, built in 1886.

Whether you're an avid hiker or looking for a casual stroll, Minoo Park has something for everyone. Its trails begin with a 2.7km paved walkway, and is easily accessible from the main train station.

Minoo waterfall is only a short distance along the trail, and is an incredible spot for taking photos and enjoying the beautiful red foliage during autumn.

The walk around Minoo Park should take around 45min, with a major draw

card being the **Ryuanji Temple**, located at the midpoint of the walk.

Osaka Castle and gardens

Osaka Castle sprawls across sweeping grounds, which cover over 60,000 sqm. It's filled with over 600 cherry trees and boasts a moat tall enough to give a view over most of the city.

The grounds are a sight to behold during spring, when cherry blossoms frame the castle in bright pink flowers. At any time of the year though, it's still a popular walking spot for locals and tourists alike.

Entry to the castle grounds is free. Make sure you allow a few hours to walk the perimeter of the castle. To discover the full history of this remarkable building, visit the eight-storey museum inside the castle – the view from the top is well worth the climb.

> 66 99
>
> The grounds of Osaka Castle are a sight to behold during spring, when cherry blossoms frame it with bright pink flowers.

Nightlife

Dotonbori

This is the night-time heart of Osaka, with its neon lights and hundreds of eating and drinking establishments.

The canal that runs through the centre of the district is flanked on both sides by cafes, restaurants, bars, and street food stalls. You'll also find the **Shochikuza**, a large old theatre that showcases traditional arts like kabuki.

The **Zuboraya restaurant** is an *izakaya* (Japanese gastropub) specialising in *fugu* (blowfish). The potentially poisonous fish is displayed in tanks out front. Inside, the atmosphere is convivial. *Fugu* is great paired with *nihonshu*, or sake, and there's plenty on offer here.

Another favourite is **Kanidoraku**, the famous crab *izakaya* with its enormous, moving 3D crab, beckoning patrons from the street. Crab dishes go well with both *nihonshu* and Japanese beer. For dessert, try a crepe from **Alcyon Creperie**. The "tanuki" crepe has chestnut cream, toasted soy powder, and vanilla ice cream and is our favourite here.

Hozenji Yokocho

The name of this little street in the **Dotonbori** neighbourhood, a few blocks south of the canal, means "Hozen Temple Alley." The narrow pathway is choked with tiny bars and restaurants, many hung with paper *chochin* lanterns, and runs up to the **Hozen Temple**.

Though the alley is only 80m long and 2.7m wide, it hosts over 50 shops. Try *katsudon* (pork cutlet over rice) sold at a shop of the same name, or *okonomiyaki*

> **The canal that runs through the centre of the district is flanked on both sides by cafes, restaurants, bars, and street food stalls.**

(savoury cabbage pancake with a wide range of toppings) washed down with *shochu*, the Japanese distilled liquor.

Shinsekai

Shinsekai means "new world" in Japanese, and this old neighbourhood looks like what someone envisioned the new world to look like, 100 years ago.

The **Tsutenkaku Tower** rises above the city at the centre of the district. The nostalgic neighbourhood is a good place to enjoy street food like *kushi-katsu* (deep fried food on sticks), whiskey highballs in tiny dive bars (be sure to order Suntory, which was born and bred in Osaka), looking at old-fashioned movie posters and antique pachinko parlours.

Try *takoyaki* (bits of chopped octopus in a savoury batter grilled in globes the size of a golf ball) at **Aji no Daimaru**, where you can choose your own toppings. Order some Asahi beer to go with it — the famous beer company originated in Osaka. There's also a spa complex with real hot spring water and corny themes called **Spa World**, where you can relax by getting naked with strangers.

OSAKA

One-Day Itinerary

Breakfast at Osaka castle

Early morning stillness at **Osaka Castle** belies the intense crowds later in the day. Sit on a bench by the moat with some coffee and a packet of hotcakes from a nearby *conbini* (convenience store), with a view of stone walls so massive they seem to blur in the distance.

Dotonbori and Shinsaibashi shopping

The inner city neighbourhoods around Namba are excellent for random exploration and discovery. Within the narrow alleys are some of the city's most multi-cultural dining options – from New Zealand meat pies, to Persian kebabs, with lots of local fare in between.

Walk along the canals of **Dotonbori**, and see **Glico man**, newly resplendent in LEDs; hunt for second hand shops, and vinyl records within **Shinsaibashi**; and then start heading south through the

array of kitchen utensils in **Sennichimae Doguyasuji Shopping Street**, enroute to **Namba Parks**. Snack on *takoyaki* (octopus in spheres of savoury batter).

Down-time at Namba Parks

Take some time to chill in **Namba Parks**. This shopping district was beautifully designed with nature in mind, and green terraces break the otherwise grey city sprawl. Nod off watching a movie, or refill your reserves in **Bagel and Bagel**. Surprisingly enough, its main menu item is bagels, but they also bake brownies, cookies, and muffins.

City walk: Shitennoji to Shinsekai via Tobita Shinchi

As the afternoon cools, head south, and experience a time-warp to Japan's Showa era. The districts around **Tennoji** are older and poorer, and many shops

❝❞ As the afternoon cools, head south, and experience a time-warp to Japan's Showa era.

50

have not been renovated since the 80s.

First stop, **Shitennoji**, Japan's oldest Buddhist temple located 2kms south east of Namba Parks. Check the calendars around your arrival date, as this beautiful temple hosts the occasional flea market. Important seasonal festivals like the goose-bumps inducing **Doya Doya Matsuri** are also held in February, when high school aged boys, clothed only in loin cloths, run through freezing showers of water flung on them by their sadistic teachers.

Thrills of a different sort abound in **Tobita Shinchi**, 2kms south. It's the largest prostitution district in Osaka, and very different to **Kabuki-cho** in Tokyo. Young women wait in the doorways, watched over by elderly *mama-chan*. Foreigners are not encouraged, and neither is photography, however walking down the street is tolerated.

Head directly north towards the iron beacon of **Tsutenkaku**. The tower stands within **Shinsekai**, a neighbourhood that exudes a Blade-Runner-esque, slightly tattered glitz. It's the best place in the city for *kushi-katsu* (deep-fry on a stick) restaurants, and for a very reasonable price, you can eat your fill and drink some beers to an excellent day in Osaka.

> ❝❞
> **In Shinsekai, for a very reasonable price, you can eat your fill and drink some beers to an excellent day.**

Getting around

Rail and metro
The best way to get around Osaka. Purchase an unlimited, 1-day pass at vending machines in any of the subway stations from ¥800 per day.

Buses
Like most major cities, buses are available, but they aren't very easy to use for non-Japanese speakers.

Taxis
Taxis are the most expensive mode of transport in Japan. Think twice before hopping in!

OSAKA

Japan's third largest city, Osaka is a major economic hub with welcoming people, a rich and varied food culture, flashing neon signs, plus a lot to see and do.

HIGHLIGHTS

Bunraku
A traditional form of Japanese puppet theatre.

Dotonbori
The best place to enjoy regional dishes.

Okonomiyaki
One of Osaka's specialties.

Osaka Castle
A must-see destination and popular cherry blossom viewing spot in Osaka in Spring.

BUNRAKU

Bunraku is a traditional form of Japanese puppet theatre, which has been registered by UNESCO as a world-intangible cultural asset. Bunraku performances can be watched at the National Bunraku Theatre in Osaka.

DOTONBORI

Filled with bars and restaurants, flashy Dotonbori is probably the best place to enjoy regional dishes.

OKONOMIYAKI

Okonomiyaki (savory pancakes) is one of Osaka's specialties and one can tailor it to their own taste with various toppings and ingredients. This is reflected in the name 'Okonomi' meaning 'to one's liking'.

OSAKA CASTLE

Timeless, majestic, beautiful, a must see destination. The Castle Park is a popular cherry blossom viewing spot in Osaka in Spring.

TENJIN FESTIVAL

The Tenjin Matsuri festival held at the Tenman Shrine in Osaka on 24 and 25 July is one of the three great festivals of Japan and includes traditional performances,
a night-time procession of about one hundred illuminated boats, and a firework display.

OSAKA ACCOMODATION

OO OOOOO *Based on 916 reviews

INTERCONTINENTAL HOTEL OSAKA
3-60 Ofuka-Cho Kita-Ku,
Osaka, Osaka Prefecture, 530-0011
Tel: +18778595095

Review by TripAdvisor Traveller **Mars707**
Reviewed 7/01/2017

Stayed there for 2 nights at the end of our Kansai trip and had a wonder-ful experience there. The location is great for shopping and dining. About a 10-min walk from JR Osaka, and a bit more for the subway. And I suggest you follow the directions on the hotel website for access from the train sta-tion for your first visit as the station is huge and can be confusing. IC Osaka is at the far end of Grand Front Osaka.

Check-in was smooth but not...

OO OOOOO *Based on 1117 reviews

OSAKA MARRIOTT MIYAKO HOTEL
1-1-43 Abenosuji, Abeno-ku,
Osaka, Osaka Prefecture, 545-0052
Tel:

Review by TripAdvisor Traveller
CarolineTsang
Reviewed 7/01/2017

The hotel is located at a very conve-nient location, it is just above a major rail station (Tenoji) and the shopping mall provides good choices of food. The hotel lobby is on the 19th floor. The guest room have a fantastic view! It feels spacious, modern and really comfortable. The staff we met are very helpful. Compared with other hotels of similar grading in the more central part of Osaka, I consider this one very valued for money. Certainly,...

OSAKA
ACCOMODATION

*Based on 1280 reviews

THE ST. REGIS OSAKA

3-6-12 Hommachi, Chuo-ku, Osaka,
Osaka Prefecture, 541-0053 Tel:
+81662583333

*Review by TripAdvisor Traveller catrinat777
Reviewed 6/01/2017*

My husband and I stayed here for 3 nights
and got a room w the east view! It was
amazing!! We loved all the pow-er shower
jets and comfortable bed! The butler
service provide us with din-ner
recommendations and directions on how
to get to the Osaka Aquarium Kaiyukan by
train. The instructions were detailed. It was
accompanied with photos and walking
instructions. I love the Butler Service!

The Hotel is directly above the Hom-machi
station. It is ...

*Based on 828 reviews

FRASER RESIDENCE NANKAI OSAKA

1-17-11 Nambanaka, Naniwa-ku,
Osaka, Osaka Prefecture, 556-0011
Tel:

*Review by TripAdvisor Traveller antonm85
Reviewed 5/01/2017*

We stayed at Fraser Residences for 3 nights
on our first trip to Osaka. It was fantastic.
We were worried as everyone who had told
us about Japanese ac-comodation said it
can be quite small but the rooms at Fraser
Residences were quite spacious, even with
a living area and a full kitchenette and with
all utensils, pots, crockery etc. Lots of
cupboard space and everything sup-plied
that you can think of. Rooms are very clean
and the bathroom great (...

OSAKA
WINE & DINE

*Based on 428 reviews

KIJI UMEDA SKY BLDG.

1-1-90 Oyodonaka, Kita-ku, Umeda Sky
Bldg. B1F Takimi KojiOsaka, 531-0076 Tel:
+81 6-6440-5970

Review by TripAdvisor Traveller mamamia0
Reviewed 3/01/2017

Nice place to visit especially during sunset.
A lot of locals gather for coffee chit
chatting and most tables taken half hour
before sunset. Breathtaking views during
light and dark can be ap-preciated. A must
if in Osaka.. at least you have seen one of
the 20 must see buildings in the world!

*Based on 271 reviews

MATSUZAKAGYU YAKINIKU M, HOZENJI YOKOCHO

1-1-19 Namba, Chuo-ku,
Osaka, Osaka Prefecture, 542-0076
Tel: 06-6211-2917

Review by TripAdvisor Traveller
S G
Reviewed 8/01/2017

Melt in your mouth black wagyu is best
with Jap draft!!!
The fried rice was sinful and soooo worth
the calories!
I would eat here again and again!

OSAKA
WINE & DINE

Based on 710 reviews

ICHIRAN DOTONBORI

7-18 Soemoncho, Chuo-ku, 1F Osaka,
Osaka Prefecture, 542-0084 Tel: +81
6-6212-1805

Review by TripAdvisor Traveller
Miles S
Reviewed 7/01/2017

Not the best ramen I've had, but quite good. Really cool ordering system that allows for customization of your ramen bowl. Super quick service. Definitely not good for groups. About 10 single person stalls available at this place.

Based on 462 reviews

KANIDOURAKU DOTOMBORI-HONTEN

1-6-18 Dotombori, Chuo-ku, Osaka,
Osaka Prefecture, 542-0071 Tel: +81
6-6211-8975

Review by TripAdvisor Traveller
Peter T
Reviewed 6/01/2017

It is one of the most popular crab restaurants in Japan. There are other many crab restaurants in Hokkaido but not in Osaka. I visited this restaurant almost every time I am in Osaka. Two things to bear in mind. First, I took about three hours in the wait line. So, I went there in the afternoon and they gave me a number and approx. time, say 745pm. I come back at 745pm and I get into my table right the way. It was kind of reservation. Next, the a...

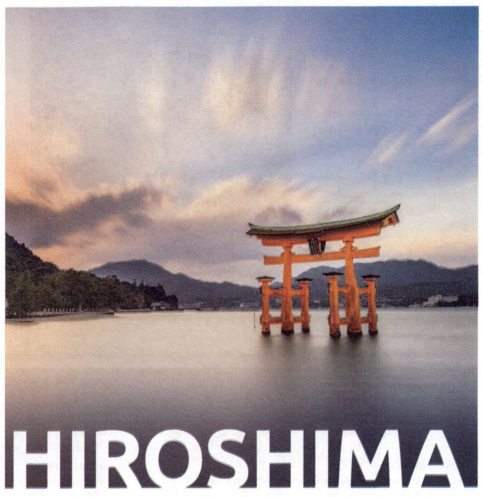

HIROSHIMA

T hough most well-known for its tragic past, today, Hiroshima is one of Japan's most vibrant cities. Many tourists visit the city on day trips (it takes just 90 min from Osaka on the shinkansen), but stay a weekend and you'll discover a treasure-trove of historic sites, awe-inspiring museums and some of the wildest nightlife in Japan. It's time to rediscover this infamous city.

59

Must See and Do

Hiroshima Peace Memorial

Visit the UNESCO World Heritage site, **Hiroshima Peace Memorial**, a.k.a. the A-Bomb dome. It's located along the **Motoyasu River** and also near **Hiroshima Peace Park**.

The fact that the shell of this iconic building still stands today symbolises the resilience of Hiroshima after the attack in 1945.

Hiroshima Peace Park

History gets pretty real in the park's **Peace Memorial Museum**, with exhibits of burnt-out school uniforms of kids who disappeared after the attack and photos of *hibakusha* (people who were exposed to the bomb's radiation).

If this sounds like too much, there are many other monuments in the park to pay your respects, like the **Children's Peace Monument**.

Itsukushima

This island, also known as **Miyajima**, is home to the **Itsukushima shrine** and its famous red *torii* gate. Both appear to float on the sea at high tide.

Be sure to try the *momiji manju* (maple leaf-shaped cakes) and fresh-grilled oysters.

Heads up: deer roam the streets freely and although they're pretty tame, they will steal your food when you're not looking!

Momijidani Park

The perfect times to visit the park is during autumn, when the *momiji* (Japanese maple) trees turn a vibrant red, or during spring, when the cherry blossoms are in full riot.

From the park, you can hike or take a cable to the top of **Mt. Misen** for panoramic views of the Seto Inland Sea.

Hiroshima Castle

Although the original was destroyed during WWII, the renovated structure is pretty impressive.

Inside, learn about Hiroshima's history, try on samurai gear, or trek to the top of the castle for expansive views of the city.

Afterwards, trawl the grounds for the perfect picnic spot or feed the koi and turtles that live in the moats around the castle.

> **"** History gets pretty real in the park's Peace Memorial Museum, with exhibits of burnt-out school uniforms of kids who disappeared. **"**

with carrots, take the ferry from Tadanoumi Port (2h from the city) and prepare to be mobbed!

Ninoshima

Ninoshima is another island worth checking out. Accessible by ferry from Hiroshima Port, it's home to **Aki no Kofuji**, the island's own version of **Mt. Fuji**.

It's definitely off-the-beaten-path, having once been the site for quarantining Japanese soldiers and atomic bomb victims during WWII.

Cycle around the island's peaceful trails and bring some snacks since there aren't any restaurants here.

Shukkeien Garden

About 15 mins walk from Hiroshima Station is **Shukkeien Garden**, a compact, Edo-period landscape garden. Although smaller than other famous gardens in Japan, Shukkeien Garden is perfect if you want to escape the crowds for a while.

Stroll along the paths and contemplate the miniaturised landscapes of forests and mountains to find your Zen in the middle of the heaving city.

Okunoshima

Does an entire island overrun with bunnies sound like heaven to you? If so, to get your furry fix, head to **Okunoshima**, found off the mainland. Although the rabbits were first brought here to test poison gas during WWII, today, they're perfectly harmless. Stuff your pockets

"

Does an entire island overrun with bunnies sound like heaven to you? To get your furry fix, head to Okunoshima.

Nightlife

Get serious about Sake

Did you know that Hiroshima's nightlife is the place to try world-class sake? They're so serious about this drink that every October, the **Saijo district** hosts a huge sake festival where you can drink to your heart's content.

Popular bars and clubs

Even if the Japanese staple isn't your favourite tipple, there are lots of places to cosy up with a glass of wine or whiskey and munch on some *yakitori* (Japanese-style meat on a stick).

Start at **Nagarekawa**, Hiroshima's ultimate party district. Wander around the streets to check out beer gardens, *izakayas*, bars, nightclubs, pachinko parlours, hostess clubs… you name it! If you're looking for some decent craft beer, try **Raku Bar**, the self-styled Japanese craft beer café. They offer *nomihodai* (all you can drink) so you try as many craft beers as you like. Be sure to try *Kaigunsan*, craft beer from **Kure City** in Hiroshima Prefecture.

If you're after a more rock 'n roll atmosphere to swill your whiskey or *shochu*, **Koba** cranks out the tunes until late. Bom-san, the bar's musician-owner, makes you feel right at home, as though you've been friends for ages. Koba also hosts live music on occasion.

With a name like **Wonderful Joke Bar**, you're bound to be curious. This tiny bar has an intimate feel and there's free karaoke if you're into belting out 80's hair band anthems or some sweet Taylor Swift.

> "This tiny bar has an intimate feel and there's free karaoke if you're into belting out 80's hair band anthems."

Looking for something more familiar? **Molly Malone's** is the closest thing you'll get to an authentic Irish pub – owned by an Irish man – in this part of Japan. Popular with expats and locals, you're bound to meet an interesting crowd here on any night. Catch up on the latest footy or rugby match and get this – you can even get a Sunday roast here!

Other hot spots in town: **The Shack, Bar Pretty, Southern Cross, Le Jyan Jyan, Tropical Bar Revolucion**.

Must-try restaurants

You can't leave Hiroshima without trying its claim-to-fame – *okonomiyaki*. This savoury pancake is a one-size-fits-all crepe, overflowing with noodles, meat, seafood, vegetables and any other ingredient you want, all smothered with a savoury-sweet sauce.

One of the best places to chow down on this awesome deliciousness is **Okonomimura**. In this four-storey building, you can choose from loads of *okonomiyaki* restaurants. Follow the crowd (or your nose), pull up a chair to the hot griddle (watch those elbows), and let the chef do his thing.

Another famous place to try *okonomiyaki* in Hiroshima is **Micchan**. This restaurant claims to be one of the city's first, serving up the dish since the 1950s. Although there are many in town, locals swear by the one in **Hatchobori**.

On the other hand, if you're feeling adventurous and you're after a spicier version of the Japanese dish, head to **Lopez Okonomiyaki** for jalapeno pepper-style *okonomiyaki*.

One-Day Itinerary

Spend the morning at Hiroshima Peace Park

Hiroshima's peace park is a truly serene and contemplative space located in the centre of Hiroshima. Start here in the morning to avoid the crowds. Designed by architect Kenzō Tange, this area was once a busy part of downtown Hiroshima, flattened by the 1945 Hiroshima bombing. The park is a space to memorialise the victims, and for contemplating world peace.

Next, take a walk through the **Hiroshima Peace Memorial Museum**. The museum is dedicated to educating the world, with hopes for a more peaceful future through the legacy of those affected by the 1945 atomic bomb.

Hiroshima Castle, built in 1958, is a complete reconstruction of the 1590's original that was flattened in the atomic bombing. Complementary to the Peace Memorial Museum, it now

serves as exhibition of Japan's history up until 1945.

Art walk at Hiroshima Museum of Art

Located opposite Hiroshima Castle, the **Hiroshima Museum of Art** features a collection of classical, modern, and contemporary works from both Japan and abroad. This impressive collection is complemented by a rotation of world-class temporary exhibitions that ensure there is always something to see.

On your way to the **Shukkei en garden**, stop off for lunch at one of the *okonomiyaki* restaurants to sample the local specialty: *Hiroshima-yaki*.

An afternoon of Zen

Dating back to 1620, this famous garden is known for its miniature natural landscapes. Stroll through the garden along the path, taking you past

> ❝❞
> The Hiroshima Peace Memorial Museum is dedicated to educating the world, with hopes for a more peaceful future through the legacy of those affected.

63

multiple teahouses, offering perfect views of the traditional Japanese garden aesthetics.

Famous for its beautiful floating *torii* gate, **Itsukushima shrine** is the must-see centrepiece of **Miyajima island**. Built along the shore of the island, the centuries-old shrine is Miyajima's namesake, translating to 'Shrine Island.' Regarded as a holy Shinto site, the shrine consists of multiple buildings that appear to float on the water during high tide.

Behind Itsukushima shrine lies **Momijidani park** at the base of **Mt. Misen**. Cultivated during the Edo period when the saplings were planted along the **Momijidani river**, the park is one of the most beautiful maple leaf parks in Japan.

Cap off the night with fresh seafood

Oysters are one of Hiroshima's most celebrated local produce, so no trip to the prefecture is complete without a tasting. Enjoy one of the various restaurants on **Miyajima** serving the island's famous barbecued oysters.

The famous **Yakigaki-no-hayashi** serves oysters in every way imaginable.

Note that the last JR ferry leaves at 8:15pm, but the last Matsudai Kisen ferry is not until 10:15pm.

> **Oysters are one of Hiroshima's most celebrated local produce, so no trip to the prefecture is complete without a tasting.**

Getting around

Rail and metro
Tokyo and Hiroshima are also connected by the JR Tokaido/Sanyo Shinkansen.

Buses
Ferries are the best way to get to different islands. There are overnight ferries for longer trips.

Taxis
These are the most expensive mode of transport in Japan. Think twice before hopping in!

HIROSHIMA

Located in the Western Honshu region of Japan, Hiroshima is a modern, cosmopolitan city rich in history, with excellent cuisine and a bustling nightlife. With six rivers flowing through the city, Hiroshima is known as the 'The City of Water'.

HIGHLIGHTS

Atomic Bomb Dome
A must-see for any visitor to Hiroshima.

Hiroshima Peace Memorial Park
Promotes world peace.

Miyajima
Enjoy mountains, sea and red shrine buildings.

Shukkei-en Garden
Lose yourself in the compact and beautifully landscaped.

ATOMIC BOMB DOME

A must-see for any visitor to Hiroshima, the World Heritage Listed Atomic Bomb Dome was the only building left standing in the area after the bomb exploded on 6 August 1945.

PEACE MEMORIAL PARK

Visit the 120,000-square metre Peace Memorial Park which commemorates the atomic bombing of Hiroshima and promotes world peace.

HIROSHIMA STYLE OKONOMIYAKI

Try Okonomiyaki Hiroshima style: savoury pancake filled with layered ingredients like cabbage, beansprouts, shrimp, meat, and egg.

MIYAJIMA

Enjoy mountains, sea and red shrine buildings on the island of Miyajima, said to be one of the three most beautiful sights in Japan.

SHUKKEI-EN GARDEN

Lose yourself in the compact and beautifully landscaped Shukkei-en Garden with its valleys, bridges and islands designed in 1620, said to be modelled on the world-famous scenic beauty of Lake Xihu in Hangshou, China.

HIROSHIMA
ACCOMODATION

*Based on 785 reviews

SHERATON GRAND HOTEL HIROSHIMA
12-1 Wakakusacho, Higashi-ku, Hiroshima, 732-0053
Tel:

Review by TripAdvisor Traveller **souths70**
Reviewed 8/01/2017

My wife & i stayed here for 3 nights in a corner king room. The location is fan-tastic, as it is about a 50m walk from where the airport bus drops you off, & right next to the rail station if coming by train. We found it to be an ideal lo-cation for exploring this wonderful city.

Check in was fast & friendly. We were allocated a room on the 18th floor which had fantastic views over the city. The room was quite large by Japanese standards (40m2) & ...

*Based on 230 reviews

HIROSHIMA WASHINGTON HOTEL
2-7 Shintenchi Naka-ku, Hiroshima, 730-0034
Tel:

Review by TripAdvisor Traveller **Jordan R**
Reviewed 5/01/2017

By far the biggest room we've had while in Japan (for a reasonable price at least. Comfy bed (western queen size too). Good breakfast with both Japanese and western options. Huge bathroom. Right in the heart of the shopping district and only a 10-15 minute walk to peace park and muse-um. I would recommend this hotel to anyone.

HIROSHIMA
ACCOMODATION

*Based on 1306 reviews

HOTEL GRANVIA HIROSHIMA
1-5 Matsubaracho, Minami-ku,
Hiroshima, 732-0822
Tel:

Review by TripAdvisor Traveller motemburst
Reviewed 3/01/2017

The Granvia is a modern hotel attached to the Hiroshima railroad sta-tion, which makes it hugely convenient for rail travelers (just about everybody, right?) My 2 adult children and I rented a 3-person room for 3 nights. It was bright, modern, and fresh, but very tight (it was really a 2-bed room into which a 3rd bed had been crammed). But while the room was tight, it was no more tight that I've come to expect from Japanese urban hotels. The t...

*Based on 983 reviews

RIHGA ROYAL HOTEL HIROSHIMA
6-78 Motomachi, Naka-ku
Hiroshima, 730-0011
Tel:

Review by TripAdvisor Traveller
whitebrooke
Reviewed 8/01/2017

The RIHGA Hotel is very close to attractions around Hiroshima if you do not mind walking rather than catching transportation. The rooms were clean and comfortable with very friendly staff. The buffet also provided both Japanese and Western breakfast foods.

HIROSHIMA
WINE & DINE

*Based on 251 reviews

HASSEI

4-17 Fujimicho, Naka-ku,
Hiroshima, 730-0043 Tel:
+81 82-242-8123

*Review by TripAdvisor Traveller Jorge Luis H
Reviewed 8/01/2017*

It's true, one of the best Okonomiya-ki
restaurants in town; when it's not crowded,
service is fast and good, if it is several
people waiting all slow down. Bad thing is
place is so small so I recommend going
weekdays and if you have to go at weekends
go there by lunch.

*Based on 22 reviews

ROOPALI WAKAKUSACHO

14-32 Wakakusacho, Higashi-ku,
Hiroshima, Hiroshima Prefecture,
Tel: +81 82-264-1333

*Review by TripAdvisor Traveller
DCTravelers69
Reviewed 4/01/2017*

We ate here because we stayed at a hotel
very close and we were looking for good
Indian food. The food was fabulous--not
greasy at all(!) and the naan was incredible
(get the coconut, you won't regret it). We
had a lovely meal and the staff were very
attentive. Highly recommend!

HIROSHIMA
WINE & DINE

*Based on 23 reviews

NAGATAYA

1-7-19 Otemachi, Naka-ku,
Hiroshima, 730-0051
Tel: 81822470787

Review by TripAdvisor Traveller **TuhoJuho**
Reviewed 7/01/2017

Excellent spot for the Hiroshima local delicacy okonomiyaki. Rarely any Japanese restaurants have even concidered vegetarian and even vegan options on their menu but this place has.

A great place to go with a group of people with different eating habits and diets. And it's convenietly located close to the Peace park.

It's fun to observe the cooks preparing the meals, too! Good atmosphere and suoer friendly staff!

*Based on 115 reviews

GUTTSURI-AN

1-36 Tannacho, Minami-ku,
Hiroshima, 734-0034
Tel: +81 82-256-1520

Review by TripAdvisor Traveller **Bjarni B**
Reviewed 2/01/2017

went there late december. amazing food, the atmosphere fun. The lady in the front was imformativeand fun. just great! you can take bus 12 from down-town really easy and saves money. no that this place is expensive.

OKINAWA

From the moment you arrive, you'll see why Japan's southernmost prefecture is known as "The Hawaii of Japan". With its sun-blessed, tropical weather, and endless white sand beaches, you'll never want to leave. Made up of more than one hundred subtropical islands – collectively known as the Ryukyu islands and stretched over 700km of ocean – this is where the Japanese come to get away from it all. There's pristine oceans and coral reefs, teeming with life, for divers. There's rugged terrain, covered in lush vegetation, for hikers and mountain-bikers. Okinawa is an adventure traveller's dream-come-true. Get ready to fall in love with Japan's best-kept secret.

Must See and Do

Explore Shuri castle

To get there, catch a train to Shuri station, and take a short walk to the castle. **Shuri Castle** will keep you occupied for half a day, so make sure you give yourself plenty of time.

There are warning signs for poisonous *Habu* snakes for a reason – leave them undisturbed and you'll escape unscathed. After buying your pass, explore this unique structure, check out the gorgeous rooms, and marvel at the lacquer hardware.

Don't miss the traditional performances too, where you might even be bitten by a performing *shisa* (lion-dog) for good luck!

Go for a snorkel or dive the Kerama islands

For day trips and short getaways, visit the **Tokashiki, Zamami, Aka** and **Geruma islands**. There are plenty of marine adventures like snorkelling and diving, which are world-class, or just relax on any of the white sand beaches and admire the clear blue sea. Camping on **Zamami** is popular too, and provides access to uninhabited islands.

Learn traditional crafts at Miyakojima

Friendly **Miyakojima** is renowned for its beaches and reefs, including Sunayama, Araguska, Yoneha, and Maehama. For the culture-vultures,

don't miss the botanical gardens. Here, you can make traditional crafts, feed and ride Miyako ponies, and explore a small jungle. Downtown is good for hand-crafted souvenirs and sampling the local delicacies – Miyako soba and fresh sea grapes are a must! At Miyako airport, you can rent a car or scooter if you haven't organised one beforehand.

Visit Okinawa's picture-perfect Yaeyama islands

This gorgeous chain of islands is just a short flight from Naha city. If you're looking for pristine beaches, wild flora and fauna with local charm and flavours, this is the place to be. The islands include **Ishigaki**, and **Yonaguni**. A couple of nights' stay at each is highly recommended.

Monkey around Ishigaki

Hiking, visiting beaches, and eating

> " Here, you can make traditional crafts, feed and ride Miyako ponies, and explore a small jungle.

OKINAWA

ishigaki beef are the must-do experiences here. Cars and scooter are the recommended way to get around the island – you can rent these when you arrive.

Take some time to stop by the lookout points and explore the local crafts shops and restaurants. Have a picnic overseeing either **Hirakubo** or **Uganzaki Lighthouse**. Immerse yourself in local culture and have fun with monkeys at **Ishigaki Yaima Village**.

Advanced divers can also swim with manta rays – all the local dive shops regularly have tours, so pick your favourite. For longer stays, hop over to the islands of **Taketomi, Iriomote**, and **Yonaguni**.

Ancient civilisations in Yonaguni

A curious underwater formation is the subject of debate amongst archaeologists (and truthers) everywhere. Some say they are ancient ruins, others claim aliens. Killjoys say it's just a natural formation.

Decide for yourself with an unforgettable close-up dive (make sure you're properly licensed), or view it via glass-bottom boat.

Conquer Mt. Omoto, Okinawa's highest peak

At 582m above sea level, **Mt. Omoto** on **Ishigaki island** takes about 2h for a return trip and the views are well worth the effort. It's pretty small compared to other treks on mainland Japan, but it's still challenging, so it's best suitable for experienced hikers.

> **"**
> **Some say Yonaguni are ancient ruins, others claim aliens. Killjoys say it's just a natural formation.**

Hiking boots are a must, as the journey will involve crossing a river and passing a waterfall, but the views at the summit are just incredible.

Take a leisurely hike up Mt. Gusuku

This distinctive rocky mountain of **Iejima** is only a 30min ferry from mainland Okinawa. The course will have you passing through *torii* gate and visiting a sacred shrine. It's suitable for hikers of all levels. Though hiking boots aren't required, enclosed footwear is advisable.

Take more than a few selfies with the panoramic views at the top and make sure you quench your hard-earned thirst afterwards at a local eatery downtown.

Try Okinawa's soba noodles, which are thicker than udon noodles, and often served with pork belly.

75

Outdoor Activities

Live the Island life on Kerama Islands

As the closest group of islands off mainland Okinawa, you can easily enjoy a day trip or a short stay here compared to the southern-based islands. **Tokashiki, Zamami, Aka**, and **Geruma** make up this veritable smorgasbord of sightseeing and adventure activities. From viewing humpback whales to camping, and of course – diving, snorkelling, and sunbaking – you'll always be entertained. At night, enjoy the beautiful fireworks or stargaze with friends over a local beer or sake.

See the postcard-worthy beaches of Miyakojima

Get ready to try snorkelling, diving, stand-up paddle boarding, kayaking, and even banana-boating. There are also a tonne of beaches that are the stuff of postcards like **Sunayama, Maenohama, Yoshino**, and **Aragusku**.

For something a little different, go exploring around the **Boraga "pumpkin cave"**.

Feed the fishes in Ishigaki

With a coast dotted with beaches, the reef of **Yonehara** is definitely a highlight. Here, friendly locals will advise you of the top snorkelling spots, and may even give you some food. It's not for you – bring it with you snorkelling so you'll be surrounded by hungry and colourful tropical fish.

Meet the cheeky residents of **Monkey Forest** at **Ishigaki Yaima Village** and don't forget to try their local signature dish, *ishigaki* beef.

Diving with aliens in Yonaguni

This is the southern-most island of the **Yaeyama islands** (in fact,

> Meet the cheeky residents of Monkey Forest at Ishigaki Yaima Village and don't forget to try their local signature dish, ishigaki beef.

the whole of Japan). A mysterious underwater rock formation is a must-see attraction here. One theory claims that it was formed naturally, while others say it was man-made.

Either way, definitely go have a look and decide for yourself. Even if you don't dive, you can view this unusual wonder on board a glass-bottomed boat.

Hike Mt. Gusuku

This unique landmark on **Ie island** has a breathtaking trail, suitable for all levels of hikers.

It winds past a shrine lined by several **torii gates**, all the way up to a summit with spectacular views of the town below, the deep blue sea, and mainland Okinawa. There are steps all the way to the top, so while hiking shoes are not necessary, enclosed shoes are highly recommended.

Ryukyu islands diving

Diving is no doubt one of the main attractions of Okinawa. Speak to any of the local (accredited) dive shops about your level of experience and what you'd like to see and they can point you in the right direction. You can greet a rainbow of exotic fish, and perhaps even a turtle or two. Head towards **Ishigaki** for a manta ray experience, but make sure you bring your diving license!

Spider loop mountain biking area

Gearheads can challenge themselves with this track based on mainland Okinawa. Check out shorter trails like **The Chute** and **Spider Alley** (don't worry, the giant spiders are harmless, despite their threatening appearance). To enjoy the bumps and thrills, make your way to **Kaneda**, which is accessible by car.

Nightlife

Izakayas

These cosy Japanese gastro pubs are the heart of Okinawa nightlife, and they're chock full of character. Here you'll find Japanese co-workers or friends sitting cross-legged on *tatami* mats enjoying a wide range of shared dishes. We recommend ordering the local specialty – Okinawa soba, of which every *izakaya* will have their unique, secret recipe.

Some *izakaya* offer all-you-can-eat or all-you-can-drink specials for a set fee. There's no need to search for a specific *izakaya*, just head to the nearest one, point at a few items on the picture menu and enjoy.

Drinks

For beverages, the local Orion beer reigns supreme. For something stronger, try the *awamori*. Although similar to sake, *awamori* is made with Thai rather than Japanese rice, and served with a jug of cold water and ice.

You pour and mix your own drink, and traditionally the drink of your superior. For those looking for something alcohol-free, try the *sanpincha* (jasmine tea) or one of the local fruit juices, *acerola* (similar to cranberry) or *shikuwasa* (similar to a lime).

In the capital, Naha City, **Sakaemachi Arcade** is filled with small bars where you can meet the locals.

Naha Nightlife

Naha is home to some excellent nightlife. **The Dojo Bar** is owned by karate black belt and British ex-pat, James

"There is a wide range of cuisine. Diners can choose from Thai, Indian, Nepalese, Mexican, Turkish, Greek and Italian.

Pankiewicz. There's great food and drinks, and is often filled with martial artists making their pilgrimage to the birthplace of karate.

Parker's **Mood Jazz Club** serves up fine wines with live jazz, while **Gold Disc** caters for those who long for the days of rockabilly and Elvis. At **Hateruma** on **Kokusai Street**, there are nightly performances of traditional Okinawan music, with songs played on the three-string *sanshin*.

Chatan

About 45min north of Naha is the beachside entertainment area of **Chatan**. In close proximity to the U.S. military base, there is a wide range of international cuisine. Diners can choose from Thai, Indian, Nepalese, Mexican, Turkish, Greek, and Italian restaurants. The Okinawa Brewing Company's **Mihama Café**, has the best selection of craft beers on the island.

Your night wouldn't be complete without a line dance and a ride on a mechanical bull, so pull on your boots and head over to **Nashville Restaurant and Rodeo**, "The place to git yer country on."

OKINAWA

One-Day Itinerary

For a quick stop-over

If you are travelling elsewhere and Okinawa is just a stopover, we'd suggest to stay close by the airport. Chances are, this might be in **Naha city**. There's plenty to do here and getting around is easy with busses, monorails, or taxis. To utilise your time well, a taxi will be your best bet. Though it's the costlier option than the others, you can get to exactly where you want to go.

Head to **Hokusai Street** in Naha, which is lined with souvenir shops and places to try delicious local cuisine. Next, hop in a cab and head to **Shuri Castle**, the palace of the Ryuku Empire.

If you've got time afterwards, head to **Okinawa World** – just 30min from **Shuri Castle** – where you can take a look at the museum, explore the natural cave and grab a bite to eat. It's also a great place to grab some handmade souvenirs for the family!

For a day-trip

If you've got 24 hours in Okinawa, WE HAVE GOOD NEWS! There's a lot more time to squeeze in a bit more. Hire a car and drive to the northern part of the island, where you'll find beautiful beaches and less tourist crowds.

Head to **Motobu Peninsula**, a beautiful region surrounded by crystal clear ocean. Visit **Okinawa's Churaumi Aquarium**, which is one of the largest in the world and a must-see. While you're here, take a walk around **Ocean Expo Park** to learn about local sea-life.

Don't forget to stop at **Nakijin Castle** too, one of the largest castles in Okinawa. Depending on your budget, we'd recommend staying at one of the resorts up this end of the island – it will be well worth the money and give you more time to explore this untouched part of Okinawa.

66 99

Drive to the northern part of Naha island, where you'll find beautiful beaches and less crowds.

Getting around

Monorail
The monorail only navigates around Naha. Though the transportation is efficient, it can be confusing for anyone that doesn't know their way around, or speak the language.

Taxi
There are plenty of taxis around, but these will leave you out of pocket.

Planes
From the mainland, Okinawa is an easy plane ride to the city of Naha. Islands closer to mainland Okinawa are accessible by boat, whereas another flight is required for islands further south.

Buses
Though buses connect within the islands, these aren't very easy to use for non-Japanese speakers.

Sapporo, in Hokkaido's west is the largest city on the island. The 1972 Winter Olympic Games were held here and nowadays the nearby Niseko is a popular destination for Australian skiers. Sapporo is well known for its annual Snow Festival, ramen and beer.

HIGHLIGHTS

Odori Park
Filled with flowers, trees and fountains.

Sapporo Beer Museum
Opportunity to taste a variety of beers.

Sapporo Snow Festival
Delightful collections of intricate illuminated snow statues.

Snow
Excellent skiing with 15 metres of dry, powder snow falling on Niseko each year.

MOERENUMA PARK

Surrounded by a marsh, Moerenuma Park has a circumference of about four kilometres and sculpture on a grand scale, with installations including a glass pyramid where performances are held.

ODORI PARK

Odori Park, which stretches about a kilometre and-a-half in the centre of the city and is filled with flowers, trees and fountains, provides welcome respite from the crowds.

SAPPORO BEER MUSEUM

The Sapporo Beer Museum gives visitors a guide through the process and history of beer making in Hokkaido, as well as the opportunity to taste a variety of beers.

SAPPORO SNOW FESTIVAL

See delightful collections of intricate illuminated snow statues in Odori Park in Sapporo City during this festival, which is visited by about two million people every year.

SNOW

Close to Sapporo, the resorts of Niseko and Furano offer excellent skiing with 15 metres of dry, powder snow falling on Niseko each year.

SAPPORO
ACCOMODATION

Based on 56 reviews

JR TOWER HOTEL NIKKO SAPPORO
2-5 Kita 5 Jo Nishi, Chuo-ku,
Sapporo, Hokkaido, 060-0005 Tel:

Review by TripAdvisor Traveller
Sarah F
Reviewed 8/01/2017

The other reviews were accurate and I was prepared for a small room. I will add that the bathroom was spacious by comparison. Traveling there from the airport on the JR express train is convenient and straightforward. The meeting I attended had one event in the hotel and the catered food was excellent. I ate the breakfast buffet one day and it was just what I'd expect in a nice international hotel. I also tried the traditional Japanese breakfast ...

Based on 98 reviews

VESSEL INN SAPPORO NAKAJIMA PARK
1-2 Minami 9-jo Nishi 4, Chuo-ku,
Sapporo, Hokkaido, 064-0809 Tel:
+81345891560

Review by TripAdvisor Traveller
P7004UAelainel
Reviewed 7/01/2017

The staffs of the hotels is sincere and helpful(especially Amy Yamaguchi, she helped so much for the reserva-tion for the dinners in the restaurants) the rooms is tidy and the breakfast is quite delicious, the location is very convenience to the subway station. only 1 minutes walk, very easy to find .The price of this hotel is very valuable, Hope will be here again very soon

SAPPORO ACCOMODATION

Review by TripAdvisor Traveller William R
Reviewed 8/01/2017

Large and nice rooms, excellent breakfast, friendly and helpful staff. Located 3 subway stops from Sapporo Station and a block and a half from Nakajima Station. Lots of restaurants, etc. within a short walking distance.

⊙⊙ ○○○○○ *Based on 926   reviews

IBIS STYLES SAPPORO

3-10-10 Nishi, Minami8Jo, Chuo-ku, Sapporo, Hokkaido, 064-0808 Tel:

Review by TripAdvisor Traveller
meganhilderson
Reviewed 8/01/2017

Located 5 minutes walk from JR station this hotel with roof top Japanese Baths is excellent. Breakfast offers a wide selection of food both Western and local. Rooms are big with every-thing you'd expect.

⊙⊙ ○○○○○ *Based on 1111 reviews

CROSS HOTEL SAPPORO

2-23 Kita 2 Jo Nishi, Chuo-ku, Sapporo, Hokkaido, 060-0002
Tel:

SAPPORO
WINE & DINE

OOOOO *Based on130   reviews

SOUP CURRY & DINING SUAGE
5-chome Minami4jo Nishi, Chuo-ku,
Sapporo, Hokkaido, 064-0804
Tel: +81 11-219-6274

Review by TripAdvisor Traveller
RedRoseLaughs
Reviewed 6/01/2017

Saw this restaurant on Trip Advisor and
being fairly new to dining out in Japanese
cities found our way her with the help of
MapMe. Eventually found the right place
which like a lot of eateries in Japan cities is
hidden away located at the top of a a very
uninspir-ing staircase.
Queued for around 15 minutes to get into
the restaurant and were eventu-ally seated
at the counter. Would have preferred to sit
at a proper table but didn't really spoil o...

OOOOO *Based on62   reviews

NEMURO HANAMARU JR TOWER STELLAR PLACE
2 Kitagojonishi, Chuo-ku, 6F Stella Place
Sapporo, Hokkaido, 060-0005
Tel: +81 11-209-5330

Review by TripAdvisor Traveller
andrewhedgehogging
Reviewed 7/01/2017

At the recommendation of my brother-in-
law, we ventured to this sushi place on our
first day in Sapporo. We waited close to
half an hour and this was like 5pm! The
queue was long and we were given a seat
at the bar and not the conveyor, where we
had to actually put in orders as opposed to
just swiping plates off the belt. It was a
little intim-idating at first because we
spoke little Japanese, but the menu had
English and pictures.

The sushi was...

SAPPORO
WINE & DINE

⭐ ○○○○○ *Based on 943 reviews

SAPPORO BEER GARDEN

9-2-10 Kita7Jo Higashi, Higashi-ku,
Sapporo, Hokkaido, 065-0007
Tel: +81 120-150-550

Review by TripAdvisor Traveller
Seow Poh L
Reviewed 7/01/2017

Our family of 4 had a great time at the
museum, garden and cafe cum souve-nir
shop next to the museum.
The museum packs info on the begin-
nings and progress of the beer factory.
Definitely worth the repeat visit when
we're back in Hokkaido. For the beer if not
for anything else!

⭐ ○○○○○ *Based on 25 reviews

ROKKATEI, SAPPORO HONTEN

6-3-3 Kita 4 Jonishi, Chuo-ku,
Sapporo, Hokkaido, 060-0004
Tel: +81 11-261-6666

Review by TripAdvisor Traveller Annie C
Reviewed 25/07/2016

Rokkatei Sapporo Honten is centrally
located in Sapporo city. It is a 10-sto-rey
building but normally not entirely opened
for public access in normal days. The
Gallery and small garden are nice places
to stop by and do not request an
entrance fee.

There is one café and one bistro-like
restaurant. The Café mainly serves drinks
and desserts. The restaurant offers more
choices of a meal. The Café is simple,
decorated almost all in white. Uten...

GUIDE TO PRACTICAL JAPANESE

Japanese is the official language of Japan, and is spoken
by more than 130 million people. Little is known when the language first appeared in Japan. Although there is some evidence that it was spoken sooner, substantial texts did
not appear until the 8th century. Old Japanese was heavily influenced by Chinese in the Heian period (794-1185). Between 1185-1600, changes in the language brought Japanese closer to the modern language and European loanwords first appeared. After the end of Japan's self-imposed isolation from the world in 1853, the flow of loanwords from European languages increased, and there are now in particular quite a number of Japanese words that have English roots.

Japanese has a complicated writing system consisting of two sets of phonetic syllabaries and thousands of Chinese characters called "kanji". The syllabic writing systems
"hiragana" and "katakana" were created out of "kanji",
and today Japanese is written with a mixture of the three. Japanese texts can be written in Western style, i.e. in horizontal rows from the top to the bottom of the page, or in traditional Japanese style, i.e. in vertical columns from the right to the left side of the page. Both writing styles exist side by side today.

One of the most fascinating things about the Japanese language is the extensive grammatical system dedicated to expressing politeness and formality – this includes 'polite language', 'respectful language' and 'humble language'. Which you use is determined by the social status of yourself and the person that you are speaking to – so different words and expressions are used when talking to an unknown person or a superior, as opposed to when talking to a child, family member or a close friend. There are for example more than five different words for the English word "I", which are used depending on the context.

Compared to many other languages, Japanese has relatively few sounds, and pronunciation is fairly easy. However, there are many homonyms, i.e. words that are pronounced the same way, but have different meanings.

Here are a few words and phrases that may come in handy while you are away:

Hello
Kon'nichiwa

Good morning
Ohayō gozaimasu

Goodbye
Sayōnara

How are you?
Ogenki desu ka?

I'm fine
Genki desu

Excuse me (to get attention)
Sumimasen

Sorry
Gomen'nasai

Please (when asking)
Kudasai

Thank you
Arigatō

Yes
Hai

No
Iie

I don't understand
Wakarimasen

Do you speak English?
Anata wa eigo o hanasemasu ka?

Where is the ...?
... wa doko desu ka?

My name is ...
Watashi no namae wa ... desu.

What is your name?
O namae wa nan desu ka?

Where are you from?
Shusshin wa doko desu ka?

I'm from...
Watashi wa ... no shusshin desu.

How much is this?
Kore wa ikura desu ka?

I'm just looking
Miteiru dake desu

What time is it?
Ima nanji desu ka

Can I sit here?
Koko ni suwatte mo iidesu ka?

I would like
O onegaishimasu

I'm allergic to...
Watashi wa ... no arerugii ga arimasu

I'm a vegetarian
Watashi wa bejitarian desu

Cheque, please
Okaikei onegaishimasu

With (something)
Issho ni

Without (something)
Nashi de

When?
Itsu

Where?
Doko

Who?
Dare

What?
Nani

You
Anata

I
Watashi

Foreigner
Gaijin

Okay
Hai

Beautiful
Kirei

Market
Ichiba

Restaurant
Resutoran

Menu Menyū	**Chicken** Toriniku
Bar Bā	**Pork** Butaniku
Coffee Shop Kissaten/café	**Seafood** Shīfūdo/ Kaisambutsu
Tea Ocha	**Eel** Unagi
Coffee Kōhī	**Fish** Sakana
Beer Bīru	**Salmon** Sake
Water Mizu	**Prawn** Ebi
Knife Naifu	**Vegetarian** Bejitarian
Fork Fōku	**Vegetables** Yasai
Spoon Supūn	**Fruit** Furutsu
Bowl Bōru	**Soy sauce** Shōyu
Plate Osara	**Salt** Shio
Glass Garasu	**Spicy** Karai
Bottle Bin	**ATM** Ēītemu/ATM
Breakfast Chōushoku/Asagohan	**Bank** Ginkou
Dinner Yūshoku/ Yuhan	**Credit card** Kurejittokādo
Cold Tsumetai	**Post office** Yūbinkyoku
Warm Attakai	**Hotel** Hoteru
Meat Niku	**Room** Heya
Beef Gyūniku	**Toilet** Toire

Airport
Kūkō

Train station
Eki

Train
Densha

Subway
Chikatetsu

Platform
Hōmu

Ticket
Kippu

Taxi
Takushī

Bus
Basu

Ship
Fune

Photograph
Shashin

Temple
Tera

Shrine
Jinja

Garden
Teien/ Niwa

River
Kawa

Blossom
viewing Hanami

Cherry blossom
Sakura

Pharmacy
Yakkyoku

Help
Tasukete

Police
Keisatsu

Dangerous
Abunai

NUMBERS

1 Ichi

2 Ni

3 San

4 Shi/ Yon

5 Go

6 Roku

7 Shichi/Nana

8 Hachi

9 Ky/Kyū

10 Jū

11 Jū ichi

12 Jū ni

13 Jū san

And so on to 19...

20 Ni-jū

30 San-jū

40 Yon-yū

50 Go-jū

60 Roku-jū

70 Nana-jū

80 Hachi-jū

90 Kyu-jū

100 Hyaku

1000 Sen

91